Praise for *The Game Is Not a Game*

"Only the legendary sports writer Robert Scoop Jackson could write *The Game Is Not a Game*—a book that bristles with bracing and brutal insights that take no tea for the fever and offer no discount on truth or justice. Because he is a master of deep theory (who else could translate Michel Foucault's notion that power doesn't just hibernate in places of legitimacy but breaks out everywhere between all folk and situations), because he flings street vernacular like a grammatical drug dealer, because he is a savant of the history of sports in America, this book is an instant classic that reckons with the factors that make sports possible, and at the same time wrestles with the forces that make protest in sports necessary. *The Game Is Not a Game* is intersectional cultural analysis at its best!"   —Michael Eric Dyson, author, *What Truth Sounds Like*

"I've long said that Scoop Jackson is the Coltrane of the sports page. With *The Game Is Not a Game* he takes his skillset to a level few sportswriters—or any writers—can match. Scoop is that rarest of commodities: an original voice."   —Dave Zirin, *The Nation*

"Candid, riveting, informative—yet not surprising at all. This is Scoop Jackson we're talking about, so I expected nothing less. If you care about the sports industry . . . if you value a true, authentic, perspective on the world of sports—and about its participants—you've come to the right place. This is a treat for anyone who loves sports."
—Stephen A. Smith, *ESPN First Take*

"This is the book we've been expecting from Scoop Jackson, one of the most insightful sports journalists of our generation. With humor and brutal honesty, Scoop pulls the covers off the sports industry and the blinders off those who enable its hypocrisy."
—William C. Rhoden, author, *Forty-Million-Dollar Slaves*

"'To do this work of . . . talking candidly about race and sports, you have to realize that it's supposed to get a little messy.' In a conversation with the author, journalist Jemele Hill hits on just the thing that makes *The Game Is Not a Game* so special: Scoop Jackson is never afraid to get messy. Jackson doesn't avoid the static, he steps into it, pushing even the most woke minds to dig deeper into and think more honestly about issues of race, gender, and politics. From the NCAA to LeBron James, Serena Williams to Colin Kaepernick, Jackson uses the biggest headlines of our day to reveal that the power of sports to change the world can only be realized if the powers that run sports allow it."   —Sarah Spain, espnW.com columnist

"Scoop's contribution to sports journalism in the last three decades is unparalleled and incomparable. This leap into critical literature is not only welcomed, but crucial." —Bobbito Garcia, author and filmmaker

THE GAME IS NOT A GAME

THE POWER, PROTEST, AND POLITICS OF AMERICAN SPORTS

Robert Scoop Jackson

Haymarket Books
Chicago, Illinois

Published in 2020 by
Haymarket Books
P.O. Box 180165
Chicago, IL 60618
773-583-7884
www.haymarketbooks.org
info@haymarketbooks.org

ISBN: 978-1-64259-097-5

Distributed to the trade in the US through Consortium Book
Sales and Distribution (www.cbsd.com) and internation-
ally through Ingram Publisher Services International (www.
ingramcontent.com).

This book was published with the generous support of Lannan
Foundation and Wallace Action Fund.

Special discounts are available for bulk purchases by organizations and institutions. Please call 773-583-7884 or email
info@haymarketbooks.org for more information.

Cover design by Eric Kerl.

Printed in the United States.

Library of Congress Cataloging-in-Publication
data is available.

To Uncle Clif, Dré, Mr. Morris, Jaleen, Dedry, and Rhude Boi. Until I get there…

I learned from my enemies. Beat them at their own game.
—Killmonger in *Black Panther*

CONTENTS

INTRODUCTION

THE "RACE" TO THE FINISH

"The game is the game."

—Avon Barksdale, *The Wire*

Until it isn't. Sports has always meant many things to many people. For some they're the greatest form of recreation and entertainment; for others, one of the world's greatest sources of power; for still others, a generational saving grace. For most people, if we are being transparently honest, on some level, sports represents all three. Kareem Abdul-Jabbar wrote in the *Guardian* in an August 2018 op-ed: "To white America, the history of US sports is a rising graph of remarkable achievements of physical and mental strength. To black America, it's that, but is also a consistent timeline of attempts to silence the voices of African Americans."

Yeah, what he said.

Still, for me, over the course of a deep dive of more than twenty years into a career that has ended up being powered by sports, the responsibility exceeds the craft. I long ago chose the Spider-Man approach (*Into the Spider-Verse* version): "Everything you say and do creates an impact." I simply inserted "write" (which I tend to do obsessively) in place of "say," and treated typed words as such. Thus the journey began. And along the way I found a sense of so-called freedom.

There's ambivalence, there's uncertainty, there's plausible deniability, there's cognitive and creative dissonance. There's also a sense of mission, one that comes from an obsession with telling either a story or a side of a story that is not being told at all, or not being told truthfully or completely with all sides taken into full consideration. And that's when panic often sets in. That black panic that comes from being black while knowing how "black stories" so often get treated. Look, I never wanted any part of this book to be about me, because what I do and write is *not* about me. It's about a bigger picture—always, the bigger picture. It's about the difference between Mark Emmert, Mark Cuban, and Mark Aguirre. Between John Skipper and John Wall, Whitlock and World Wide Wes. Without even mentioning their names.

Funny thing, as much as race is at the core of almost everything in the following pages, this book *isn't* about race. You'll just *think* it is. THIS IS A BOOK ABOUT POWER. About the people that don't have it versus the people who do; how that power manifests as entitlement and respect and an authoritarian mentality; and how the abuse of that power through sports impacts and affects humanity. It's about the way sports provides a platform to the people who don't have the power, allowing them to feel, act, and react.

There comes a time when it is time for resistance, time for renewal, time for reconstruction. In America it has become evident to millions that the time is now. And if history tells us anything, if history is an indicator of how the past will reflect the future, then sports will be a part of—and play a role in—the resistance, renewal, and reconstruction of our time. But there remains a sense, *a feeling*, that people aren't really ready to deal with race, people aren't really ready to deal with power,

people aren't really ready to deal with change and challenge—
not on a direct, call-you-on-your-bullshit level. But people are
always willing to deal with sports, or to deal with issues they
aren't comfortable dealing with *through the prism* of sports. As
Rembert Browne put it, writing about Spike Lee—and in this
passage, about white America's inability to deal with Spike
Lee—for *TIME*: "Sticking to sports is one of the easiest ways
to sprint towards equality without dealing with our history."
There's the inertia of sports, and there's also the inertia of the
control of sports.

Been asked: "Is he insane?" Answered: "Yes, sir. Him is." Cut
from a different cloth. Not the best fur—not chinchilla, not cash-
mere, not kente. Cotton was the fabric that they gave we. Me
and so many others. As a sports journalist/writer/author/content
creator I've had a first-, second-, and third-hand look into the
role that power plays in both the construction and control of
organized sports, as well as all the outlets attached to it that benefit from it. Have I been a part of that attachment and benefit? Hell
yes. But I've also spent an entire career fighting against and trying to bring about public awareness of the power *true power* got.

For years I've looked at sports through a prism of power.
I've noticed how most of the people making decisions that
affect sports at the highest money-generating level are those
furthest removed from the cultural center of the games. So
often they not only look the same but *think* the same. And
what psychological damage has that done to those who *don't*
have the power? Evident but inconclusive; hard to determine.
Kind of like proving collusion or obstruction of justice against
a sitting president.

I've also learned that not having power or ownership in sports
doesn't make you powerless. My responsibility as a journalist
has been to exercise the power I do have, and to remind those

involved in sports in whatever capacity that they have power to exercise as well. We all just have to be smart about it. In sports, we can't afford to play dumb. Sports in America gives—and has given—minorities, women, the disenfranchised and disrespected leverage that is rarely afforded by any other chosen American profession. Through sports we have found a sense of freedom that is nonexistent or not accepted in other walks of life.

Which is why I've never looked at writing about sports to be a privilege. The same way I've never looked at people who make a living in sports as if it's a privilege for them. The game *is not* a game for us. It has been and remains a responsibility. *Our* responsibility. All of us—from Stephen A. to Jordan, Fritz Pollard to Floyd Mayweather, Clarence "Big House" Gaines to that one AAU coach stuck in Columbia, South Carolina, or Rapid City, South Dakota, who is not trying to get his or her team to the Jam On It Classic in Las Vegas because that coach is more concerned about teaching the team about life *through* the game than becoming a showcase *in* the game.

Because for us, "the game" *is* life.

To cry out. To resist. To complain. To right wrongs. To expose both rights *and* wrongs. To use the games played as platforms. To gain power. To assert it. To sustain it. To know, as a journalist who covers sports, that FOX pundit Laura Ingraham was speaking to me as much as she was LeBron (and all other black/ of color/woke athletes) when she said, "Shut up and dribble." Which translates to: "Shut up and write." Yes, ma'am.

To be aware that silence ain't golden. To understand that for black people in this country, basketballs do more than just bounce.

"Race is the elephant in the room, and we all understand that," Gregg Popovich, whose wokeness will be further featured in this book, stated at a press conference addressing

Colin Kaepernick and the NFL anthem protests. "But unless it is talked about constantly, it's not going get better."

Popovich went on:

> There has to be an uncomfortable element in the discourse for anything to change. Whether it's the LGBT movement, or women's suffrage, race, it doesn't matter. People have to be made to feel uncomfortable. And especially white people, because we're comfortable. We still have no clue what being born white means. ... Yes, because you were born white, you have advantages that are systemically, culturally, psychologically there. And they've been built up and cemented for hundreds of years. But many people can't look at it. It's too difficult. It can't be something that is on their plate on a daily basis. People want to hold their position, people want the status quo, people don't want to give that up. And until it's given up, it's not going be fixed.

We all know, in America at least, that what Pop describes—giving up the status quo—is something that will never happen, or at least not anytime soon. More than likely, it will remain.

Odell Beckham Jr., on HBO's *The Shop,* gave some insight.

> I tell people all the time: I really feel like a zoo animal. That's where life's gone for me. You know, you used to take your kids to the zoo and we used to be like, "I want to see the lions" or "Let's see the lions." And you go there, and the lions are laid out. You now what I mean? And it's like, "Why aren't they doing lion stuff?" Like, I've got people who call out, "Odell! Dance!" Like I'm a show punk. A show monkey or something. Like I'm a puppet. And it's like to me, that doesn't feel good. But it's like damn, that's what life's become. But can you ever really detach from that?

For most, if we are being transparently honest, on some level, whether we are playing or not, sports kinda is *exactly* like that. We are living in the world of Tim Ryan, who went on air and said that the reason Baltimore Ravens quarterback Lamar

Jackson was so good at "disguising" fake handoffs was because opposing players couldn't see the football because of the "dark" color of Jackson's skin. We are living in the world of Larry Nassar, the Michigan State University sports doctor and USA Gymnastics national team doctor who sexually assaulted many members of the USAG team (a total of over 265 women) over the course of fourteen years; and William Strampel, the MSU dean who allowed and enabled Nassar to sexually assault female gymnasts; and Steve Penny, the USAG CEO who tampered with evidence to help cover up the crimes. We are living in the world of Phil Jackson (who felt comfortable enough to call LeBron James's business partners a "posse"), Mike Ditka (who felt comfortable enough to say, "There has been no oppression [in America] in the last hundred years"), and Bobby Knight (who once felt comfortable enough to say to a female reporter, "If rape is inevitable, relax and enjoy it"); men who, because of their stature in sports, are still revered as heroes. We are living in the sports world of Myles Garrett versus Mason Rudolph, of Kaepernick versus the NFL, of the NBA versus China, of black Twitter versus Stephen A., of ESPN versus Jemele Hill, of Sam Ponder versus Barstool Sports, of pay versus play, of the reality of sports versus the reflection of society.

In the song "He Got Game," Chuck D basically gave sports a single-line manifesto: "Don't let the wins get to your head or a loss get to your heart." It's the life lesson that all athletes (and fans, owners, coaches, execs, and all the rest) have to live by and with. It's the game-by-game, season-by-season (bet-by-bet) formula for mental survival for anyone involved in sports. But for an outsider who looks between the lines where the games are played, wins aren't always victories and losses are often more than just losses. In those instances, both the heart and the head have to know when to apply that rule and when to disavow it.

THIS IS A BOOK THAT PROTESTS.

To write like I'm running out of time. To write like there are no tomorrows. To write until they call Bill Simmons "the white Scoop Jackson." To be the undefeated before The Undefeated. To meet sports on the ground level and see it for what it really is. To put a different face on what we see in sports. To challenge. To know and never lose sight of the fact that if you ever want to protest loudly, be heard, take a stance, be an activist, force change, be the leader of a cause bigger than your fame, notoriety, and promise, and have everything you scream and fight for go unnoticed, unheard, and unappreciated: write a book.

CHAPTER 1

NFL
The American Hypocrisy

"We can't have the inmates running the prison."
—Houston Texans owner Robert McNair, October 2017

The initial reaction to Bob McNair's statement was swift, but only publicly. Privately, in the October 2017 meeting with several other NFL owners, there was just a gasp. No disagreement, not one other owner checking the Houston Texans owner in the moment, telling him he can't say that. Or at least making him understand—again, in the moment—that *that* wasn't cool, not with non-owners and the media in the room, including ESPN. com's Seth Wickersham and Don Van Natta Jr. (Somewhere there had to be a "not here, not in front of them" whispered.)

No. Instead, a comfort zone in an ideology of men who own football teams—and, more importantly, players—was maintained. Many of them may not agree in totality with McNair's line of thinking, but they fully understand not only what he was saying and what he meant but also how he felt. It's a shared sentiment.

For those who follow the NFL, this is nothing new. This "controversy," as it was called—along with the spectacle of

Carolina Panthers owner "Mister" Jerry Richardson, who further validated both the theory and line of thinking at the end of the 2017 season by putting the Panthers up for sale amid accusations of sexual and racist misconduct—proved to be a continuation of issues that have come to plague the NFL, exposing the league for what it really stands for.

It is the difference between a controversy and a challenge. And history has shown us that challenge, in America, especially when it's from black people to white people and white establishments, is never recognized as such. Challenge is never the position because that is not *our* place. Instead, a challenge to authority is reduced to "controversy," a misleading label similar to the tactic of using "mental illness" to explain the actions of white mass or serial killers while labeling black or minority ones as "criminals" or "terrorists." To challenge authority in the face of what is experienced as injustice should never be considered controversial.

But let players kneel, let women's groups argue against the rampant domestic violence associated with players in the League, let a Nigerian forensic neuropathologist "challenge" the increase of head traumas among a League's workforce that has led to CTE (chronic traumatic encephalopathy), which is directly related to the suicides of several former players, including Junior Seau, Dave Dureson, Jovan Belcher, and Aaron Hernandez . . . and instantly: controversy.

Contravesty is probably more accurate when it comes to the NFL. Served with a side order of hypocrisy. Even though Roger Goodell publicly took a "concerned" tone on the handling of the players' position of not standing during the national anthem, the way the NFL has handled other issues that have confronted their operating model has been apathetic at best: drunk driving (224 arrests from January 2000 to February 2019, according to the nflarrest.com database); sexual assaults/domestic violence

(101 arrests); steroids and HGH use (somewhere between 10 and 40 percent, according to the Bleacher Report in 2015, after the League put in place an HGH testing policy in 2011 that they didn't implement until 2014); inconsistencies in their own personal conduct policies; concussion protocol and brain-injury dramas; public health insurance; and annual salary and revenue sharing complaints from a player-driven Pro Football Hall of Fame board.

Just look at the ongoing battle with player safety initiatives and what may possibly lead to the high percentage of their former players' being diagnosed after death with CTE. A study by the Boston University School of Medicine concluded in July 2017 that 110 of 111 brains of former and deceased NFL players suspected of having CTE showed signs of the brain disease.

Yet the following still happened: the NFL had a helmet sensor program in place to collect data on possible damage to players through head impact while playing. The Players Association has the Mackey-White Committee in place to push for safety initiatives such as helmet sensors. In 2015 the NFL suspended the program. According to a *Chicago* magazine article on helmet manufacturer Riddell (which provides 65 percent of NFL players with helmets) the program was suspended because the NFL "had concerns about the accuracy of the data." But the League never replaced the program with anything significant that could possibly save lives in the long term.

Litigation stands as an issue. Mistrust of what the league will do with the data stands as an issue. Ethics when dealing with the NFL always stands as an issue. The feeling is the NFL does not want the data gathered through a sensor program to be used against them in any court proceeding a player might bring against the League. Especially after the $1 billion settlement they paid out in 2016 to retired players who claimed brain injuries. So, while "tracking systems" were placed in footballs during the preseason in 2016 and "tracking devices" exist in players' shoulder pads to collect data on their speed, location, and distance covered while on the field, nothing has been done to track something far more important. *Yet*, 99 percent of the brains suspected of having CTE had it. SMH.

Just use the Rooney Rule as one of the core examples of how the NFL handles and mandates policy. The rule is in place to make sure the owners in the League at least make an attempt to consider hiring coaches of color when coaching vacancies in the NFL open. As I wrote in a piece for *The Shadow League* in 2013:

> The Rooney Rule is basically no different than the age requirement in the NBA. It's a rule put in place because the owners can't control themselves, or their behavior, when it comes to certain matters involving their teams.... Just the fact that the NFL feels the need to have a Rooney Rule forty-eight years after the Civil Rights Act was passed, speaks truth to matter and truth to power. Interpret it anyway you want, but to have a self-imposed "law" in place for the owners to even be fair across the board when looking at people as potential coaches, says all that needs to be said.

That same sentiment can be seen across the board in how the NFL handles what it considers "situations." Tread lightly, pacify, wait for the drama to die down, reinstate, and reinforce business as usual. And it works. Well, *did* work, until the anthem "controversy" took on a life of its own, birthing a "football life" the league was not expecting or prepared for.

And even though the borderline racist, inarguably cowardly policy they put in place to put an end to the anthem controversy was the quasi-opposite of the NFL norm, in many ways it reinforced that the league distances itself from serious issues and puts the onus of how those issues are handled on someone else. Even if that someone else is the franchise owners. (In May 2018

NFL owners voted to change the language in the *NFL Game Operations Manual* that "required" players to be on the field for the anthem to give players the option of remaining in the locker room. But if on the field, all players are *required* to stand or else face possible team-issued fines that can be enacted and enforced by every team individually, at their own discretion.)

Then. Came. The Settlement.

Of anything that has happened to or has involved the NFL in recent years, "throwing money" (estimated to be up $60 to $80 million dollars or as miniscule as $10 million, according to separate sources) at Colin Kaepernick and Eric Reid—to avoid entering a court battle that would have eventually exposed everything about how the league colluded against Kaep, and would have been a conspiracy theorist's wet dream when it comes to the intrinsic racism that exists among the owners—will be looked at years from now as possibly the smartest move the league has ever made. Even as it will be the one that haunts them the most. New hush money. New "we'll never admit we were wrong" money. New white power money. New slave money. New "protect the shield at all cost" money. The beginning of the "new" NFL. Ain't shit changed.

This knowledge comes courtesy of conservative columnist Wayne Allyn Root of townhall.com, in response to the anthem protests:

> Of course, the NFL's audience includes lots of diverse groups. But let's be honest. The typical NFL fan is a white, middle-class, middle-aged, meat-eating, testosterone-driven Republican (or certainly center-right).
>
> The typical NFL fan is a flag waver. They always stand for the national anthem. They wear flag pins and chant "USA, USA, USA!" They love cops and military. They're far more likely to eat hot dogs and drive a SUV, than eat tofu

and drive a Prius. In short, they are middle-class Trump voters. Not all of them. But a significant majority.

So, this isn't about free speech. This is about the survival
of your business and destruction of your brand. Someday this
will be a case study in how to destroy a brand in business
schools. Just like ESPN. Because ESPN's customers are the
same middle-class (and above) Trump voters as NFL fans.

As someone who has worked for ESPN for the last fifteen
years and written about the NFL for longer, I can say that Root
pretty much nails it. Yet he misses the greater point. In times
of crisis it is so easy for people to go the "money route" and
attach the success, failure, or meaning of a cause to a financial
bottom line. But everything ain't about money. Which might
be impossible for that "white, middle-class, middle-aged,
meat-eating, testosterone-driven Republican"—or America
itself—to understand.

The legal (please read again, *legal*) protest that took place
inside the NFL was about certain lives mattering; about certain
lives existing; about *lives,* period. Not money, not revenue; not
audience or advertising; not liberalism or populism. But corpo-
rations (independent or public companies) that generate the bil-
lions that the NFL does every year don't understand that, because
they aren't about that not-making-money life. What did Mase
say—"I don't understand language of people with short money."
That's the NFL in totality, if we are being honest. An "if it don't
make dollars it don't make sense" proposition, proven over the last
twenty years in the way they've proceeded to handle non-foot-
ball issues that have become threats to their business model and
overall line of thinking. It began with Ray Lewis striking an
obstruction of justice deal in 2000, after being directly linked
to a homicide at an Atlanta club after the Super Bowl, after he
was originally charged with two counts of murder. The league
handed him a single year of probation and a $250,000 fine. This

was followed by multiple domestic violence crimes, from Dez Bryant, Chad Johnson, and Jovan Belcher in 2012 to the video of Ray Rice punching his soon-to-be wife, Janay Palmer, then dragging her unconscious body out of the elevator, and Greg Hardy's arrest for beating and threatening to kill his then girlfriend, Nicole Holder, both in 2014; and culminating with the dismissal of Kareem Hunt from the KC Chiefs in 2018 for punching and kicking a woman but resigning only seventy-two days later, at that point from the Cleveland Browns.

Which is why Root's opinion is so trenchant. Because for the league it is all about the money, all about the brand, all about the brand connection to the consumer, which basically makes the NFL no different than most Fortune 100 companies in America. It just happens to be under a larger microscope.

A great point made by ESPN's fivethirtyeight.com came in the headline of a story: "How Do Americans Feel About The NFL Protests? It Depends How You Ask." Notice it says *"how* you ask" not "who."

And here is where one of the most recent exhibitions of NFL hypocrisy lies. When Trump called out the League, blasted the owners, called the players "sons of bitches" (which is technically a direct shot at each player's mother, but that's a whole 'nother story) and questioned Commissioner Goodell's leadership, it was then and only then that teams on the whole—including owners—came together in a display of locked arm-in-arm, kneel-in-front-of-the-flag-during-the-national-anthem unison. Narrative change. Theirs was a response to Trump, not the joining of forces to fight for and bring greater awareness to social and racial injustice.

And once that message was sent, it was back to the money. The owners crossed their own picket line and went back into "owner mode," calling out the players for their behavior during the anthem—the same players they'd just protested with. Turning their backs on the players once they let Trump and the White House know that the NFL will not be bullied or punked by anyone who is not a part of the NFL.

This quote, taken from the October 9, 2017, *TIME* cover story on Trump's fight with the NFL former Green Beret and NFL long snapper Nate Boyer, whose conversations with Colin Kaepernick redirected Kaep's positioning of protest from sitting to kneeling, hits directly at the NFL switch code: "The most frustrating thing [is] that people weren't kneeling because they believe police brutality is too high or because of racial inequality, they took a knee because they don't like Donald Trump. We're now equating the American flag with a person—not the 300 million diverse people it's supposed to represent."

Seattle Seahawk safety Doug Baldwin, who didn't join the protests until after the NFL's "Trump Week," tried to speak clarity to the Trump issue during an interview with CNN's Jake Tapper on *The Lead*.

> Jake Tapper: What is the message beyond unity? I mean, is it that President Trump can't intimidate you? Is it, you all stand together to protest racial injustice? What is that message?
>
> Doug Baldwin: Clearly, well uh, bluntly, I should say, is that we don't want this behavior to become a norm in our society. I understand that there is a lot of different opinions and viewpoints, but what I feel deep down in my heart and what a lot of people across this great nation feel deep down in their hearts is that there's been a perpetual cycle of hate being spewed from the greatest position that our country has to offer, from the White House. And, so, I think that's a direct reflection of what we are trying to accomplish with our protest, in terms of our message.

Great that the "we" Baldwin was speaking to finally included himself; too bad the "we" didn't include the owners. They'd already made their point to Trump and moved on to do what they had to do to put *their* players back in their proper place.

Seventy-five years ago, in June 1943, the Supreme Court ruled that no one can be forced to participate in patriotic rituals such as reciting the Pledge of Allegiance and standing for the national anthem. As was stated by Justice Robert Jackson: "To believe that patriotism will not flourish if patriotic ceremonies are voluntary and spontaneous instead of a compulsory routine is to make an unflattering estimate of the appeal of our institutions to free minds."

The free minds inside the NFL took an action inspired by Kaepernick's push to get the nation to find universal compassion toward resisting a systemic epidemic of legalized criminal injustice and turned it into waves of contempt. The steady three-year decline in TV ratings, which had been previously attributed to everything from the impact of cable-cutting and the new way millions are viewing sports to the backlash the league experienced for overlooking the sometimes violent and physically abusive treatment of women by players, was instead conveniently blamed solely on Americans' overall response not only to the protests but also to the NFL's handling of them. According to Trump, " ...NFL attendance and ratings are WAY DOWN. Boring games yes, but many stay away because they love our country. League should back U.S."

Lost in the uproar of "stand versus kneel" was the fact that someone—who just happened to be an NFL player—was simply trying to stand up for black people being killed by people who had taken oaths to protect them and a judicial system that was supposedly set up to act in a victim's best interest. The problem? He was doing it on two minutes of *their* time.

Which was not the way to bridge the partisan divide. Unless bridging that gap is not the plan. Unless CREAM ("cash rules everything around me") is the cream, and everything under it is irrelevant. And while the NFL wasn't the one that started the narrative of the protests being the primary reason the league's ratings were rapidly declining, NFL leadership definitely made it a point not to stop or even curb that message.

Irrational provocation. There's an art to it. The NFL has mastered it. Just look at the "mishandling" of the Kareem Hunt domestic assault situation (the league never even bothered to interview Hunt during the initial internal investigation, nor the woman he assaulted); at the "money solves everything" approach to reaching an agreement with the Players Association on the anthem-related issues; at the refusal to go to trial to prove that the league didn't collude against Kaepernick.

In contrast to Trump, the NFL is not so overt. Its subtle resistance to all things "damaging to the shield" has been, up until recently, with the Kaepernick/Reid settlement, somewhat masterful. It's owned the problems without *owning up* to anything.

Hollywood collectively has taken a stronger public stance against sexual harassment and sexual misconduct than the NFL has against domestic violence that in certain instances (Jovan Belcher and Ray Carruth) has ended in the victim's death. The Republican Party responded more strongly to Obama's presidency than the NFL has to the CTE epidemic, which is having a much larger and looming impact on society's general feeling about the league than anything that has stemmed from the anthem protests.

The NFL has publicly spoken against these issues as they have become synonymous with their league, but not in a way that has led anyone to feel that they are of primary concern. The way the league has exposed its own hypocrisy in its treatment of issues that should be considered bigger than the shield has become its internal gift as well as its external curse. It has allowed people—both diehard and casual fans—to see through the league. To draw split conclusions on what they feel the NFL truly represents.

On January 9, 2018, at 11:10 a.m., on ESPN's *First Take*, football analyst/god Paul Finebaum pretty much summed it up: "The NFL is in a freefall." Drop the lavalier. But as of February 2019, when Netflix claimed a 30 percent drop in its viewership during the airing of the Super Bowl, the freefall might be over. As Anthony Gulizia and Jeremy Willis stated in "How The NFL Took Over America in 100 Years," their August 2019 preseason feature for ESPN.com: "The NFL owns every corner of the country." This was further validated by a story in the *Hollywood Reporter*, six weeks into the 2019 season, that evidenced a 3 percent increase in viewership from the 2018 season and a 9 percent overall increase since hitting decade-low ratings in 2016. (Various reasons were stated for the bounce-back, including the growth of fantasy sports and the expansion of legalized gambling outside of Nevada.)

Policies and procedures: the two words that have been at the center of the NFL's hypocrisy, of America's league presenting itself as caring about issues like executive and coaching diversity, domestic safety, head and brain trauma, social injustice, and more, when its actions—through policies and procedures—prove differently.

Dale Earnhardt Jr., on September 25, 2017, posted a JFK quote on his Twitter account that spoke directly to the heart of how the protests should be respected: "All Americans R granted rights 2 peaceful protests Those who make peaceful revolution impossible will make violent revolution inevitable—JFK."

It was a perfect quote that should have been retweeted by the NFL to its fan base, to Trump, to the entire country. #USA. But of course it wasn't. Because too much like right is just not how the NFL rolls.

And going back to McNair's comment in the owners meeting, rooted in it rests something much bigger than just an overtly racist statement and ideology. It is the NFL's internal end game of preserving white male supremacy. Profits over principle. It's the business of football's ethic and ethnic morality. It's how the people who run the NFL sleep well at night. And the one thing that never floats well in America, not without serious pushback and provocation, is the separation of white men and their money. So if the inmates are causing that to happen, then it is the inmates who must pay.

CHAPTER 2

#THEMTOO
The UnRespected Worth
of the Woman Athlete

The Nike campaign dealt with it straight up. Perfect sentiment. Perfect statement. Perfect athlete. A simple crossing out of the word "female." That's all it was. Serena was the best person to start with. (This was even before the thirtieth anniversary campaign, led by Colin Kaepernick, who referred to Serena in the short film/commercial "Are Your Dreams Crazy Enough?" as the "greatest athlete ever.") Why not? *Unless there is a problem with a woman being considered the GOAT?* But, of course, we all know there is.

Over the course of the last decade or two, there has been no greater athlete in a major sport than Serena Williams. It's arguable, but the arguments will be short. Serena Williams is and has been both better athletically and more dominant in her sport than any male athlete has been in his. So why isn't she—and the bigger question is why will she never be—the overall sports definition of the GOAT? (This is all without taking into consideration that Serena also came back to play in a Grand Slam final within a year of giving birth.)

Why, if ESPN decided to upgrade their original *SportsCentury* series, wouldn't she finish higher than Babe Ruth, Michael Jordan, Muhammad Ali, Jim Brown, Tiger Woods, Wayne Gretzky, Jesse Owens, or Jack Nicklaus? Why, when *Tennis* magazine or the Tennis Channel does an ultimate retrospective of the game, after the greats of our time finally retire, will she not finish in the ranking of historical greatness above Nadal or Federer?

Because sexism, along with racism, greed-ism, and power-ism, remains one of the roots of universal evil. And the only true difference between sexism and the other "isms," when it comes to sports, is one of subtlety. With issues of race, greed, and power, there are degrees of nuance; with women, there is none. Most men have a different comfort zone when it comes to sexism and how it impacts women. They DGAF.

You could blame it on Danica. For she is seen as both perpetrator and the victim. She, a woman who fought to compete against men in a "male" sport and only won once. You could blame it on Kournikova. She, who never lived up to early potential (something male athletes also do, daily) and seemingly put her off-court career and interests ahead of her professional athletic aspirations. You could blame it on Serena. She, who has made the topic of her greatness undeniable athletically yet arguable professionally. As witnessed in the split-down-the-middle backlash she received after her "blow-up" during the 2018 US Open finals. Whether or not she was justified in her (over)reactions, the way she was treated by the chair umpire gave many—including Serena herself—reason to feel that a male player in the same or similar situation would have been treated differently.

But the point is that none of these women should be "blamed" for anything. The gender*ism* that gnaws at the center of all three of their careers can easily be seen as representing how the sports world views, treats, and (for lack of a worse word) tolerates the woman athlete. Even when a woman athlete way more than just holds her own in a sport the way men do. Back in 2007 I wrote a column for ESPN.com, challenging the "establishment" (that is, male-dominated) cultural bias to suggest that women are more dominant (not better or greater, necessarily) in sports than men. In the end, I concluded that the public's reaction to the column wouldn't matter, that "no one will care, because women will still be looked at in sports as less than equal"; that their "level of competition amongst themselves" would never be considered as great and too many people would feel that women athletes weren't even deserving of being in a sports conversation centered around the *elitest* level of GOATism. As expected, the column went nowhere, garnered very little external discussion. And even though two years later ESPN launched espnW.com, the thought of (a man) elevating the female athlete to equal or superior status to the male athlete was akin to treason.

While Serena seems to carry this burden on her entire legacy, other women athletes (such as Simone Biles, another great example) deal with the direct indifference of having limits and restrictions attached to how great they really are. Not only in their chosen sports but also in *their place* in all sports.

Not to pick on her, but the Danica Patrick "thing" is real. Of the three athletes referenced above, her situation speaks most unilaterally to the issue of sexism in sports because she directly competed against men. In a *New York Times* feature on her that ran the morning of her final Indy 500 race, one comment stood out. "The only thing missing was winning," Columbia University sports business professor Scott Rosner said of Patrick's career and more specifically speaking to what the outcome of her career would have been if she'd had the same success in NASCAR that she had on the Indy circuit. "What really prevented her from reaching the mountaintop was the lack of competitive success at the track."

Taken slightly out of context and looked at in the broader spectrum, the comment "the only thing missing [is] winning" to describe the success of an American athlete is the sports version of the kiss of death. Especially for a woman athlete. In sports we've cultivated a society that uses winning as the definer, the baseline from which greatness in judged. It's gotten so bad that some of the greatest current athletes are fearful of what not winning, under any circumstances, will do to their legacy; how not winning will be held against their careers and their person not just for the rest of their lives but for as long as there are debates about sports and greatness.

Not winning is never an option.

But Danica's "not winning" is unique because in her sport she went up against men. Now, the fact that—in her first Indy 500—she finished fourth and after that was able to sustain a fourteen-year, 367 dual-series career should be enough for societal, non–gender specific respect. But that would be so wrong. Competing at the highest level against male athletes wasn't enough. It made her *more* inferior in sports society's view because we now had a direct comparison between her and the hims (plural) she was competing against. That doesn't happen very often. And in Patrick's case, the fact that she didn't win was all that society and the media needed to use her as proof that women are not equal (code: inferior) to men when it comes to anything that involves athletics.

Women athletes got abilities like Beyoncé got bars. Like Hillary Rodham Clinton had votes. Like Danai Gurira stole scenes in *Black Panther*. They just *don't got* Bey's status or HRC's backing or Okoye's freedom to be both fierce *and* feminine. Or be handed the power to "guard and protect" the nation. That's the unfortunate participatory pathology.

Welcome to the world of unWokeness.

"As women we are continuously told to live in the cracks of a world shaped by and for men."
—**Soraya Chemaly,** *Rage Becomes Her:*
The Power of Women's Anger

Sociologist Nicki Lisa Cole, PhD, puts it this way: "Society and all that happens within it is made by people. Society is a social product, and as such, its structures, its institutions, norms, ways of life, and problems are changeable. Just as social structures and forces act on us and shape our lives, we act on them with our choices and actions. Throughout our daily lives, in mundane and sometimes momentous ways, our behavior either validates and reproduces society as it is, or it challenges it and remakes it into something else."

If we—society—were to apply that theory to how women are looked upon, thought of, and treated, what does that *validation* look like? In spite of talk about diversity and inclusion there doesn't seem to be a movement in place that is actually pushing *human beings* to look at one another as equals. Or anyone championing the overriding truth that diversity and inclusion by no means mean equality, or how vastly different the three concepts are.

And while most sociologists who believe in using theoretical perspectives to examine human behavior can see how both outcomes of Cole's assessments are possible, history seems to side with only one, in reality. And that is the "mundane and sometimes momentous ways our behavior… validates and reproduces society as it is."

How deep does the discrimination, the not treating or considering women in sports as equals, go? CNN presented a video photo essay on its website: "A Timeline of Social Activism in Sports." Of the fourteen photos used in the photo essay, there was only one image that even included women: a pic of

US soccer player Megan Rapinoe, taking a knee during the national anthem, prior to a match against Thailand in 2016. That's it. And even then, the inclusion of women as equals as athletes showed a woman following the lead of a male athlete.

No protest pics of Maya Moore and the entire Minnesota Lynx team advocating for "Black Lives Matter" or how "Change Starts With Us" surrounding social injustice cases; no pics of Venus Williams fighting for equal pay for women tennis players at Wimbledon and then at the US Open; no pics of pioneers like Billie Jean King or marathoner Kathrine Switzer or gold-medal gymnast Gabby Douglas or any of the women who authored Title IX and helped get it passed. Not a single one of those athlete-activists was pictured.

The problem facing activist women athletes and women in sports is that it is almost impossible to change the public; *even more impossible* to change public perception. The fight of female athletes isn't only within sports, it's against a larger, gender-dominated way of thinking and way of life.

And when the opportunity presents itself, women are not allowed the same room for error or misstep that society constantly gives to men. Simply take, as an example, boxing judge Adalaide Byrd's score card in the first Canelo Alvarez–Gennady Golovkin fight in 2017. Universally lauded by men and women boxing fans, her one "unexplainable" score card (in a fight that ended up a draw, she scored it 118–110 in favor of Canelo) re-energized the whole sexist conversation that "women know nothing about boxing" and that "women should not be involved in men's sports." If any sport in the history of sports defines "manhood" or how it's supposed to be perceived, it's boxing. And a woman judge having an off day at ringside was used to undermine women's progress in sports. Case in point: There were no women judges assigned to Canelo/GGG II.

In UFC, another "ultra-male" sport, Ronda Rousey's emotional breakdown after her first defeat to Holly Holm, in 2015, was also used as evidence of women's "weakness," even though male athletes have similar (or more outrageous) outbursts all the time.

Here's a non-sports parallel of the same paradox: Jill Abramson's ascension to the executive editor position at the *New York Times* was supposed to be a transcendent, historical moment that heralded a new way of thinking in America. In the 160-year history of the most influential (and powerful) media outlet in the world there had never a woman at the editorial helm. Finally. It smelled like equality. Abramson lasted only two and a half years, the third-shortest tenure of the nine people who have held the title since it was created at the *Times* in 1964. And even though in 2012 *Forbes* named Abramson one of the most powerful women (not people) and *Foreign Policy* named her one of the most powerful people, once removed from her post at the *Times* she unjustly became another public "example" of how women can't uphold what men uphold and have been upholding since Day One.

It is the same archaic unfairness that confronted Oprah in her initial struggles with her OWN network, which were met with the "Well, look at what Ted Turner did with TBS and TNT" narrative as a way to cast doubt on Ms. Winfrey's capability and competency. As the saying goes: same shit, just different toilet paper.

Still, the extreme and unmerciful chauvinism in sports and sports culture remains worse. Examine this as a one-shot of why women may never be considered as equals in sports, and of the mentality women are up against in sports to even receive respect: Nick Saban's on-the-field treatment of ESPN sideline reporter Maria Taylor in Week 1 of the 2018 college football season. Taylor, a former NCAA volleyball and basketball player, asked a fair question about the Tide's quarterback status, and Saban blew up at her in response. Saban represented the superior, Taylor the inferior. And even though Saban publicly apologized to Taylor the next day, the bell had already been rung: he put her in her place, and his act reinforced the dynamic of gender, power, and position.

To sit up here and act like I'm not "of it" would be a lie. Can't front, only flex. As much as I champion women in sports, when it comes to treating women's sports with the equal interest and energy that I do most men's sports, my behavior at times is two-faced. Doesn't matter what sport: gymnastics, volleyball, extreme, swimming, tennis, basketball, softball, boxing, MMA, hockey, and all other sports where women compete among women at the same level as men do, I don't "lean in" the same. Been to only two WNBA Finals while attending at least twenty NBA Finals; countless FIFA and MLS soccer games, not one US Women's soccer or other professional women's soccer matches; several NCAA sporting events, yet only one NCAAW Elite Eight game. Which makes me not much different in practice from the society I am calling out in this chapter. #ITOO am a part of the problem.

Devereaux Peters of the Washington Mystics spoke this truth in an article for *The Lilly* that registered with me because I've seen and heard it happen way too often:

> There's something about basketball that activates men's egos. It's almost as if they still consider it a sport that women should not be playing. In 2018, that is truly a tired narrative. The WNBA has existed for more than 20 years, and before that women played college and overseas basketball. Get with the times! Does this happen in other professions? I've never heard of a person saying they're a real estate agent, only to have someone snap back, "I bet I would sell more

houses than you." But I guarantee that every single woman who has played high-level basketball has been told by multiple men that she'd lose to them on the court.

The thinking that an athlete is good "for a woman" is as demeaning and degrading as saying someone of nonwhite ethnicity is a "credit to their race." It sets a lower and inferior expectation of who that person is and what their "kind" can achieve. Tragically, it happens in all walks of life, all throughout life. In the culinary and food service world it's "the best chefs are men," in the medical field it's "the best surgeons to save lives are men," in all things judicial and political it's "the most qualified to judge and govern lives are men." In the art world, the tech world, in the STEM world, in the IPO world, in the worlds of driving taxis and construction. Plenty of male real estate agents no doubt say, "I can sell more property than you, but you're good for a woman" directly to a coworker's face, strictly based on the innate belief that their "manhood" makes them superior. And she is expected to accept that as life. A life we (men) created, one we tolerate, one we still choose to live in. Another stain on the fabric. Another condescending pat on the head. As Natalie Weiner of *SBNation* beautifully said, on November 19, 2018, in the perfect sarcastic tweet about gender theory and how the world (in sports) sees, views, and treats women: "Because women are objects not people, you see."

But that's the psyche, what about the paycheck?

> Stephen Curry: I think it's important that we all come together to figure out how we can make [equal pay] possible, as soon as possible. Not just as "fathers of daughters," or for those sorts of reasons. And not just on Women's Equality Day. Every day—that's when we need to be working to close the pay gap in this country. Because every day is when the pay gap is affecting women. And every day is when

the pay gap is sending the wrong message to women about who they are, and how they're valued, and what they can or cannot become.

The thing is, this ain't about money. Per se. It's more about what money represents and how it equates to status in America; the entitlement that money affords. And although money isn't the issue, there's still a need to acknowledge the monetary gender disparity and what *that* represents.

In June 2018 *Forbes* released a list of the world's highest-paid athletes, and for the first time since they began ranking the top money makers in sports, circa 2012, no women cracked the top 100. Various reasons were cited, but at the core sits the stark reality that money is used to draw a line connecting women athletes and the lack of equality with their male counterparts.

And to further expose the lack of diversity when it comes to women finding equal footing in sports in terms of earning, of the top ten highest-paid women athletes on that *Forbes* list, eight were tennis players. Only Danica Patrick (No. 9) and badminton superstar P. V. Sindhu (No. 7) represented other sports. The male list included one boxer, three soccer players, two NBA players, two NFL quarterbacks, one tennis player, and one MMA/UFC fighter. The range of sports among the male top earners speaks to how sports across the board are respected and appreciated when men are involved as opposed to women. (This is despite the 2019 finding that the NBAPA executive director, Michele Roberts, for the year earned more than her NFL and MLB counterparts, NFLPA executive director DeMaurice Smith and MLBPA executive director Tony Clark, $2.85 million to their $2.7 million and $2.15 million, respectively.)

In a 2015 Maggie Mertens piece, asking if "Women's Soccer Is A Feminist Issue," Cheryl Cooky, a professor of women's studies at Purdue University, who coauthored a study for *Communication & Sport*, laid part of the problem on society and part at the feet of the media. "There's still this cultural investment in the idea that sport is this space wherein talent and hard work is what matters, and things like race, gender and sexual orientation don't," she said in an interview with the *Atlantic*. "The media plays a huge role in building and sustaining audiences for sport and they do it very well for men's sports and they do it horribly for women's sports."

And in professional sports, the ability to generate money plays a role in the respect game when it comes to women athletes, and it also plays a role in why women in America don't think about sports as a career the same way many men do. This presents a clear case when it comes to team sports. Because team sports (especially from a monetary standpoint) have not proven to be a pathway to glory for women who want to be professional athletes. It seems more difficult for society to accept women as equals athletically when they compete together as opposed to individually. It's peculiar. It's weird. It's sexist. And without a clear explanation as to why.

In that context, consider the US women's soccer team's public complaints of wage disparity, including their gender discrimination lawsuit against the United States Soccer Federation claiming that, in 2016, their members were paid only one-fourth of what the members of the US men's soccer team made—all while players in the NBA, on average, make one hundred times (yes you read correctly: *100x!*) more than a WNBA player.

To Steph Curry's point: as the eighth-highest-paid athlete in the world in 2018, he made $79.5 million. Serena, by comparison, as the top-grossing woman athlete in the world in 2018, made $18.1 million. *A $61 million gap.* Now go back and reread Steph's comment and see if it feels the same.

On the payor end of paychecks—the ownership end—the power that money holds in the human psyche goes deeper. Ownership, to men—especially white American men—is equated with identity. It tells them who you are and reaffirms for them who *they* are. Ownership, in all facets of life where power and entitlement are law, is used as psychological leverage: a tool to gain placement, status, and respect. And when it comes to women in sports, their overall lack of ownership plays a major role in how women are viewed.

A story on grandstandcentral.com by Dan Szczepanek addressed the issue of ownership. Stating that of the 133 teams that made up the Big 4 leagues in North American sports (NFL, NBA, MLB, NHL), only nine women (6.7 percent of teams) had ownership stake and status, as of 2018. [Note: That number increased to ten, once New Orleans Saints and Pelicans owner Tom Benson passed away and his wife, Gayle, inherited ownership of both teams in March 2018.] The article broke it down:

> Since 2000, 67 pro sports franchises have been sold, with only the Bills (them of the aforementioned wife and husband co-ownership) being purchased by a woman. That's sixty-six missed opportunities for the leagues to find and recruit wealthy women to steer their franchises.

Allow me to break it down even further: of the nine women controlling owners in professional sports in North America's Big 4 leagues, all obtained ownership through either a husband (six) or through family inheritance (three). In the minds of many men, no current woman controlling owner of a major sports team attained ownership with *her* own money. It is *he* who got them there, it is *he* who "allowed" a woman to be in that position. (This line of thinking, of course, is not equally applied to the many male controlling owners who also gained ownership through inheritance or nepotism.) How in this world of sports will women stand a chance of gaining any amount of respect if that's the reality most men live in?

An athletic director at a Tennessee high school summed up the intrinsic gender bias that women and girls have to deal with, in sports, in school, in life. After the Hamilton County school where he was also assistant principal banned athletic shorts during school, with a declaration that students wearing athletic shorts during school hours and/or during class would receive detention, Jared Hensley said the following to male students:

> I know, boys, you're thinking, "I don't understand why," "That's not fair," "Athletic shorts go past your knees." I didn't make the rules—well, I kind of did. But that's the rules, so that's just what we're going to stick to... If you really want someone to blame, blame the girls. Because they pretty much ruin everything. They ruin the dress code, they ruin— well, ask Adam. Look at Eve. ... You can really go back to the beginning of time. So, it'll be like that the rest of your life... Get used to it, keep your mouth shut, suck it up [and] follow the rules.

If anything in this chapter stands as evidence of the depth of the sexism in the male psyche that women and girls have to combat and confront, the above does. "Blame the girls." So random, but so universal. So pervasive, so comprehensive. So self-evident. Sports needs its own Carol Danvers moment. How in the hell are women supposed to gain ground or respect in and through sports when, according to a 2014 study by the Tucker Center for Research on Girls & Women in Sport at the University of Minnesota, only 4 percent of all sports media coverage in the US features women athletes?

The imprudence of Serena Williams finally being recognized in 2015 as *Sports Illustrated*'s *solo* Sportsperson of the Year should have proven enough. Singling out *solo* is significant because Billie Jean King shared the honor with John Wooden in 1972, Pat Summit shared it in 2011, Bonnie Blair shared it in 1994, Judy Brown King and Patti Sheehan shared it with six others in 1987, and Mary Lou Retton shared it in 1984, leaving Mary Decker in 1983 and Chris Evert in 1976 as the sole other stand-alone women (along with the collective US women's soccer team in 1999) to be recognized as Athletes of the Year in the seventy years of the award. (Which is almost as shameful as the fact that Usain Bolt and Roger Federer have never won it. But that falls under the category of American nationalism more than anything else. More on that and Federer in a following chapter.) For Serena finally to be recognized *twenty years deep* into her professional career is by itself a show of dishonor—not just to Serena but all women athletes—that symbolizes the ongoing struggle for equal acceptance.

While on the sports marketing side there seems to have been a push toward the empowering of the woman athlete through the adidas "Fearless AF" and "She Breaks Barriers" campaigns, along with Nike's "Better For it" and Under Armour's "I Will What I Want" messaging, there was a game-changing moment that went drastically overlooked. In July 2018, newsstands and websites saw Maya Moore's (first ever!) *Slam* cover (with "GOAT" printed on the spine), Serena's *InStyle* "The Badass Women Issue" cover, and Aly Raisman's "The Hero Issue" *ESPN: The Magazine* cover all hit at the same time. Three women from three different sports, representing "heroes," "badasses," and "GOATs," made for a unique, recognizable—unprecedented—moment.

Now, if only moments like this were "normal" or "regular" instead of unprecedented, change could follow.

Stephen R. Covey, author of *The 7 Habits Of Highly Effective People*, proposes a theory he calls "Principles of Empathic Communications":

> Empathic listening is so powerful because it gives you accurate data to work with. Instead of projecting your own

autobiography and assuming thoughts, feelings, motives and interpretation, you are dealing with the reality inside of a person's head and heart. You're listening to understand. You're focused on receiving the deep communication of another human soul. . . . In empathic listening, you listen with your eyes and with your heart. You listen for feeling, for meaning. You listen for behavior. You use your right brain as well as your left. You sense, you intuit, you feel.

Applying this to the change in thinking necessary to bring women's sports onto a level playing field with men's, it almost seems that locating "empathy" within a male-dictated world could be possible. But a Marvel Cinematic Universe–created Disneyland, *Fantasy Island*, Narnia, and a little slice of post–Kevin Spacey *House of Cards* with Robin Wright as President Underwood all rolled up into one would have to exist first. One where Beyoncé was the CEO of adidas, Jemele Hill ran ESPN, and Dr. Christine Blasey Ford testified before Congress about her professional expertise, instead of coming forward as a courageous whistleblower, only to be shamed for thwarting a man on the verge of attaining more "inherited" power.

Unfortunately the anachronistic state we exist in, as far as professional sports are concerned, is not being *seriously* challenged (yet) by those in power, or by the majority of fans. #MeToo has helped expose the truths behind assault, harassment, and disregard of woman athletes, but something additional needs to be said and done—loudly and consistently—in order for society to be aware of how our "normal" actions and thoughts are demeaning to an entire gender and their athletic achievements and contributions.

We live in a patriarchy. It's the Mr. before Mrs.; it's the taking *his* last name; it's the image of male figures as leaders of almost all regions, as primary builders and innovators; it's the number of male Supreme Court judges or Nobel Prize winners or US presidents; it's how strength and speed are equated with power and superiority, when the laws of physics clearly and consistently tell us that strength does not always equal power and speed does not always equal supremacy, and neither equals perfection or indicates dominance; it's the belief and theory that this kind of thinking is *not* misogyny; it's women's hoops still calling defense "man to man"; it's the whole "you throw like a girl" framework; it's the "all *men* are created equal" in the Declaration of Independence, written when "men" only meant white, male landowners. Simply put, it's man-ism as the default.

The historical, generational, unethical, unforgiving bottom line is this: it's *impossible* for a male-drenched and -dominated society to regard women as equal competitors and level participants. A society that does not instinctively associate women with warriors or gladiators or include them when discussing acts of battle or war. One that when it thinks of gods—an authoritative reference in sports when speaking about greatness and dominance—does not think of women. That's the regressive, phobia-based, patriarchal, privileged pathology.

Rolling Stone named Aretha Franklin the "greatest ever" in 2008. Which leaves us with this question: Will there ever be a time in sports when a media entity with equivalent power will claim a woman is the "greatest ever"?

There's only one answer: No. There's only one word for it: *UnRespected*.

CHAPTER 3

WHITE AND WOKE
The Quiet, Not-So-Risky, but So Necessary Politics of Gregg Popovich and Steve Kerr (An Abstract Myth)

"The measure of a man is what he does with power."
—Plato

"The object of power is power."
—George Orwell, 1984

"Truth is the ultimate power. When truth comes around, all the lies have to run and hide."
—Ice Cube

In the beginning there was power. There was talent, creativity, opportunity, options. At the center of it all: competition.

Innocent, pride-driven, sometimes deadly. But it was sport. It was what humans had—what humans created—to challenge another, to learn from one another, to shape what man—in man's own mind—was meant to become.

Sport helped give man voice. Like politics and protest, sport has allowed man the ability to form and shape opinion and judge one another based on our involvement and ability to be greater than the next person, to put on nonstop and ever-present display in whatever form of competition we chose. The running joke:

Q: When did man take over the world?
A: From Day 1.
Q: When did man take over sports?
A: Before Day 1.

As man's voice over the generations became louder through the mouthpiece of sports, a sub-element emerged. Leaders. Heroes. Icons. Gods and demigods. Voices of men who used either sports themselves or their stature in sports as platform and pulpit. Sports took on an extrinsic purpose. Injustice its side piece, soon to be its bastard child. Sports: the crucible for voices of reason. Curt Flood used his voice to ignite economic leverage via free agency for athletes, Muhammad Ali used his voice to challenge government on participation in war, Jon Amaechi has used his voice to put a human (male) face on homosexuality and sports at the professional level.

"Most powerful is he who has himself in his own
power."

—Seneca

"Power is a word the meaning of which we do not
understand."

—Leo Tolstoy, *War and Peace*

"We got to fight the powers that be."

—The Isley Brothers

According to Kendrick Lamar, "The yam is the power that
be." We can all smell it when we walk down the street. But
the king's name ain't Kunta. It's Waller. Historically, it's
Washington (George) and Bush (Georges). In sports, it's
Steinbrenner. It's Rupp. It's Knight. It's Ditka. It's Saban. The
power belongs to men who preside over sports in positions of
authority; men, mostly white, who have become worshipped
for their abilities to lead. Men associated with winning, men
who play chess with other men's lives, men who often *think* a
certain way. The way they are taught, raised, and conditioned
to think benefits their power and their positions in sustaining
and exerting that power.

Among those men, two happen to be walking a different
path. Men who don't see the world as most others in their "powers that be" positions do. Both Gregg Popovich (San Antonio
Spurs head coach) and Steve Kerr (Golden State Warriors head
coach) have publicly made it very clear that power in America
as is is not something they are proud of or proud to be a part of.

Steve Kerr Quote 1 (San Jose Mercury News, February 17, 2017):

We have a president who has no regard for compassion or empathy, in the most important leadership position in the world. The most important thing in being a leader—as a parent, a teacher, a coach—is dignity for the position you are in, empathy for others. You're trying to help people. And it feels like we're in a time where our leader is just ridiculing constantly—on Twitter, whether it's making fun of a handicapped person, or tweeting about how horrible *Saturday Night Live* is, the failing *New York Times*, casting the media as the opposition. This is not leadership. And I think people realize that. It should not matter if you are a conservative or a liberal. It's about leadership, it's about compassion and dignity and character and treating people the right way. That's leadership. It's terrifying we have someone in office who espouses none of that. I think that's why I'm encouraged by all the people who recognize that, are appalled by it and are trying to do something.

Steve Kerr Quote 2 (San Jose Mercury News, September 21, 2016):

No matter what side of the spectrum you're on, I would hope every American is disgusted with what's going on in the country, what just happened in Tulsa two days ago with Terence Crutcher. Doesn't matter what side you're on on the Kaepernick stuff, you better be disgusted with the things that are happening. I understand people who are offended by his stance, maybe they have a military family member or maybe they lost someone in a war and maybe that anthem means a lot more to them than someone else. But then you flip it around and what about non-violence protests? That's America. This is what our country is about. It's a non-violent protest. It's what it should be about. So I think Colin has really clarified his message over the last couple weeks. I would think that something similar will happen in the NBA. And as I said, no one has to be right, no one has to be wrong. I would hope everyone respects each other's points of view. There are valid points of view on both sides. But as I said, I think Colin, when he met with Nate Boyer, decided to kneel instead of sit, acknowledged his respect for the military and really clarified his message that this is about unarmed black people being killed indiscriminately around the country, and it just happened two days ago. That's the message. That's what matters. The other stuff, you can talk about all day. Nobody's right, nobody's wrong. But that matters and everybody should be trying to do something, whatever's in their power.

Steve Kerr Quote 3 (Sports Illustrated, September 19, 2018):

First of all, I think the times have changed, and the times call for it… I think where the NBA's gone right is the leadership works closely with the players, whereas the NFL has conjured up ways to create this false patriotism and pandered to their fan base, and they can't really figure out what to do, whether the players should stand or kneel. Whereas the NBA got out in front of all of it just by being partners with the players and being pretty much up front and outspoken themselves, going back to the Donald Sterling stuff a few years ago and really beyond.

Gregg Popovich Quote 1 (The Undefeated, November 9, 2016):

A pretty good group of people immediately thought he was disrespecting the military. That had nothing to do with his protest. In fact, he was able to do what he did because of what the military does for us. Most thinking people understand that, but there is always going to be an element that wants to jump on a bandwagon and that's what is unfortunate about our country. It's easier for white people because we haven't lived that experience. It's difficult for many white people to understand the day-to-day feeling that many black people have to deal with. I didn't talk to my kids about how to act in front of a policeman when you get stopped. I didn't have to do that. All of my black friends have done that. There's something that's wrong about that, and we all know that.

Gregg Popovich Quote 2 (Newsday, *January 17, 2018*):

I think it's unimportant to have to do it for a reason other than it's a good idea and making sure we all understand there are social issues in the country that can be addressed, should be addressed. That's the reason why you do it, not necessarily because it's a certain individual. Whether it's honoring the military or the LGBT community, it doesn't matter. We have a responsibility and a platform. So, to use it is wise and responsible.

Gregg Popovich Quote 3 (The Undefeated, *November 9, 2016*):

It's pretty obvious that the national stain of slavery continues to permeate our social system in this country. People want to ignore it, don't want to talk about it, because it's inconvenient.

The outspokenness and frankness. The realness and openness. The courage and temerity. All beautiful to witness. All necessary in order to make the change they seek or to force a

change unwanted. But theirs is without risk. For they are protected. They are not threats to themselves or to others around
them. The fearlessness in politicizing moments of subsistence
and subjects of discomfort is rare for those like them. The
rule to Kerr's and Popovich's "whites in power" exception is
too often the half-woke, half-hearted stances similar to Philadelphia Eagles head coach Doug Pederson's "Can't we all get
along" position, taken in the eye of the NFL's protest storm.

> If they wanted to do something teamwide, I would defi-
> nitely be for that. I think it just shows unity, and there's no
> division that way. And I think it sends a great message that
> from our standpoint and the National Football League and
> the platform and as individuals, we love this country and
> what it represents and the flag and the national anthem and
> everything. Listen, we're not perfect, obviously, and for us
> to stand sort of united that way would be—I would be OK
> for that.

Coach speak at its coach speak finest. There's safety in both
those words and approach. Most coaches know this, most live
on the side of that safety. A safety that never ignites, instigates,
or forces change; a safety that is the byproduct of minimizing
overt racism and covert majoritarian rule. Safety that secures
their power and position. When Popovich said "inconvenient"
he pretty much summed up the way American tolerates the
issues and lives of those who aren't white and male.

Decades before Pop and Kerr challenged the power set-up
in America, author and city planner Arnold Schuchter (who
is white) did a Pop/Kerr before Pop/Kerr in the book *White
Power/Black Freedom*. Putting the mirror up to America, challenging it to see what he knew to be America's truth:

> If a single factor, such as birth or color, governs the way and
> the place in which a person will spend his life, so that under
> ordinary circumstances a person cannot change the basic

features of his existence and his class status, that society is stratified by a caste system. The United States has an open-class system, except for lower-class Negroes whose lives, in terms of education and occupational mobility as well as family resources, are extremely limited and negatively reinforce each other. As a minority color-caste, Negroes do not have the power to break out of their relatively rigid class situation. The perpetuation of white–Negro caste relationships reflects the status quo of power distribution in the social structure.

That was 1968. In the fifty-one years along the way, others connected to sports—those who weren't athletes but had some skin in the games—joined the choir. The anti-Schotts, the anti-Sterlings. The modern day Branch Rickeys. In this modern era of sports, Pop and Kerr have personified the "Anti." Antiestablishment. Anti-privilege. Anti-Trump. Anti-conservative. Anti-right wing. Anti-segregation-via-power coaches, whom Americans have rarely seen or heard because they weren't associated with winning, the white-and-woke members of American sports society who in the past were probably silenced. At this stage of the game, neither Popovich nor Kerr can be silenced. It's too late; they've both amassed too much power through winning and too much visibility through respect and differentiating themselves from every other coach who looks like them. Nike should create a T-shirt for both of them to wear on the sidelines during games and in press conferences that says "I'm Not Woke, I'm Wide Awake."

> "I have said, the first thing is to be honest with yourself. You can never have an impact on society if you have not changed yourself."
> **—Nelson Mandela**

> "White privilege is a manipulative, suffocating blanket of power that envelops everything we

know… It's brutal and oppressive, bullying you into not speaking up for fear of losing your loved ones, or job, or flat (home). It scares you into silencing yourself: you don't get the privilege of speaking honestly about your feelings without extensively assessing the consequences… challenging it can have implications on your quality of life."

—**Reni Eddo-Lodge,** *Why I'm No Longer Talking to White People about Race*

"Silence is the ultimate weapon of power."

—**Charles de Gaulle**

An awakening. Of sorts.

There's an elephant in the room that I've been thinking about a lot over these last few weeks. It's the fact that, demographically, if we're being honest: I have more in common with the fans in the crowd at your average NBA game than I have with the players on the court.

And after the events in Salt Lake City last month, and as we've been discussing them since, I've really started to recognize the role those demographics play in my privilege. It's like—I may be Thabo's friend, or Ekpe's teammate, or Russ's colleague; I may work with those guys. And I absolutely 100 percent stand with them.

But I look like the other guy. And whether I like it or not? I'm beginning to understand how that means something.

What I'm realizing is, no matter how passionately I commit to being an ally, and no matter how unwavering my support is for NBA and WNBA players of color. . . . I'm still in this conversation from the privileged perspective of opting in to it. Which of course means that on the flip side, I could just as easily opt out of it. Every day, I'm given that choice—I'm granted that privilege—based on the color of my skin.

When Kyle Korver wrote that in his step-into-the-light piece for *The Players Tribune* entitled simply "Privileged," he decided that being silent was no longer an option. His piece resonated as a wake-up call to America from one of its own, which it was. Of course, it reached semi-viral status and transcended the confines of the world of sports. It spoke directly to the power that his friend (Thabo Sefolosha, who was "mistakenly" beaten by NYC cops when he and Korver were both members of the Atlanta Hawks in 2017), his teammate (Ekpe Udoh, who's been witness to and an indirect victim of racist rants), and his colleague (Russell Westbrook, who, during a game against Korver's Utah Jazz squad, was told by a fan to "Get down on [your] knees like you're used to") were denied in specific situations when their hue and heritage was held against them, and it spoke directly to the power Korver possesses by being white in America.

But long before Kyle Korver got to speak his piece, Popovich and Kerr had spoken theirs. Laying foundation and framework in the NBA, they provided the necessary white shoulders for Korver to stand on so that he could speak so freely and comfortably.

And in the terms of power that comes with being who he is in America: Korver gets it.

> "Imagination is not only the uniquely human capacity to envision that which is not, and therefore the fount of all invention and innovation. In its arguably most transformative and revelatory capacity, it is the power that enables us to empathize with humans whose experiences we have not shared."
>
> **—J. K. Rowling**

> "It is not power that corrupts but fear. Fear of losing power corrupts those who wield it and fear

of the scourge of power corrupts those who are
subject to it."
                    —**Aung San Suu Kyi**, "Freedom of Fear"

"Absolute power was not meant for man."
                    —**William E. Channing**, *Thoughts*

"You see what power is, holding someone else's
fear in your hand and showing it to them."
                    —**Amy Tan**

Coach Muffet McGraw had her own Popovich/Kerr moment
right before the 2019 Final Four, where her Notre Dame basketball squad won one of two games that would have given
her a third national championship.

"When you look at men's basketball and 99 percent of the
jobs go to men, why shouldn't 100 or 99 percent of the jobs in
women's basketball go to women? Maybe it's because we only
have 10 percent women athletic directors in Division I. People
hire people who look like them. And that's the problem," she
said. She stood on a platform so strong that the NCAA WBB
(woman's basketball) put out a tweet of Muffet's observations,
calling her "a voice for women. A voice for women in sports."

"When is it going to become the norm instead of the exception?" Muffet asked out loud. "How are these young women
looking up and seeing someone that looks like them, preparing
them for the future? We don't have enough female role models.
We don't have enough visible women leaders. We don't have
enough women in power."

Her voice, her power. No different from the men's, still
earned through sports. Unlike Korver but much like Kerr
and Popovich, Muffet's voice comes from a successful coach's
position of power. She can flex, and people react—*then* act.

They walk her walk for her. A pied Pippa. The sports version of Alexandria Ocasio-Cortez, who will more than likely be treated like Christine Blasey Ford. Exercising her power of progressivism while knowing that what she says out loud will be silenced by the yam.

> "Nearly all men can stand adversity, but if you
> want to test a man's character, give him power."
>
> **—Abraham Lincoln**

> "Power is my mistress. I have worked too hard
> at her conquer to allow anyone to take her away
> from me."
>
> **—Napoleon Bonaparte**

Here's a reach: the woke whiteness of Kerr and Pop has, to a degree, emboldened others in positions of power to flex the truth as they see it. Damn the risk of offending half their audience and half the country. Chris Evans, who portrays the most American of American superheroes in the Marvel Cinematic Universe, Captain America, felt comfortable enough to call out not just President Trump but New England quarterback and NFL GOAT Tom Brady for his association with Trump. "I'm just really hoping he's not a Trump supporter. I'm just hoping he's one of those guys that maybe supported him and now regrets it. Maybe he thought it was going to be different—and even that bothers me—but maybe there's a chance he just thinks Trump's an absolute dumb shit, which he is. If he doesn't, if he's still on that Trump train, I might have to cut ties. It's really tough. I think maybe a couple of years ago I might have tried to pull some mental gymnastics to compartmentalize, but I don't know if I can anymore. So I'm hoping he's woken up."

Not saying that Pop and Kerr gave birth or a platform to those thoughts (Trump has the power to ignite that all by himself), but the freedom inside that comment—*especially centered around an American god like Brady*—has Pop and Kerr written all over it. Yeah, it's a reach. But still…

> "The world does not need white people to civilize others. The real white people's burden is to civilize ourselves."
> —**Robert Jensen,** *The Heart of Whiteness: Confronting Race, Racism and White Privilege*

> "In the general course of human nature, a power over a man's subsistence amounts to a power over his will."
> —**Alexander Hamilton**

> "As a matter of fact and experience, the more power is divided the more irresponsible it becomes."
> —**Woodrow Wilson**

This shit *ain't new*. The power, the distinguishing of power, the dispensing of power, the use of it. By whites. In sports. In life. In America. But let us not get it twisted. The reverence of Pop's and Kerr's "quiet" (meaning: their voices have not drowned out their careers such that America sees them as with their color or their inherited privilege.) They and the few others in similar positions who have followed their outspoken leads have not been able to say what they've been able to say— and suffer minimal public or media-driven consequence in the process—because they are white. They are able to stand *on* what they stand *for* openly due to their history of winning and continual ability to win. Same with Muffet McGraw. Same with any coach who has amassed the respect that comes with winning in sports in America. Being white is a bonus. An added uniqueness. Winning one-ups race, sometimes gender, often class, on occasion politics. A coach—especially a white one—who sets a standard for winning is in most cases the most powerful person in their respective sport. More powerful than an owner; just as powerful, sometimes, as the league they coach in. In sports, winning allows (damn near) all to take shape, exist, and often be excused. It equalizes and allows indifference (damn near) more than right or wrong. So the next time you look at Gregg Popovich or Steve Kerr and think of how cool and dope it is for them to be so candid, blunt, forthright, and brave because they are white, pause, gather yourself, and iden-tify that it's their winning that allows them to be heard, not the entitlement they happened to be born in to. Winning gives them power in sports that the color of their skin cannot equal. And winning *is* the pillar of power, right?

Here's what I know for sure: If Popovich were black, he'd be labeled a race-baiter, difficult, his credibility disregarded and authority dismissed. But he's not, so privilege does have a good side. Winning protects him from being labeled a white ver-sion of all the aforementioned. And until America has a coach of color in any sport that wins at the pace, level, and degree that Pop has over his twenty-two-year head coaching career in San Antonio (or Nick Saban's in Alabama, Geno Auriem-ma's in Connecticut, Bill Belichick's in New England, and so on), this labyrinthine theory and belief that winning "protects" an individual from the customary consequences of unreserved and brazen social activism will hold.

In an August 2017 column on the privilege of whiteness in sports for the *New York Daily News*, Carron J. Phillips ended with this reassurance: "Because when White privilege is used for good, it can go a long way in shining a light on the many injustices that occur on a daily basis that some choose to simply ignore."

This defends the use of the word "necessary" in this chapter's title and explains why it is vital when speaking of the *necessity* for whites in sports to speak both up and out in order for change to occur. In order for the landscape to lean toward level or for power to discover the humane side—as opposed to the controlling side—of humanity there has to be white steel in these hours of chaos. Power speaks, people listen. Privilege speaks, people hear. It all depends on the messenger.

"The ultimate value of life depends upon awareness and the power of contemplation rather than upon mere survival."

—Aristotle

"Power up with the word
I got it from my God
He said a good shepherd don't trip over what they heard"

—Rapsody, "Power"

"You got the power to let power go?"

—Kanye West, "Power"

CHAPTER 4

COLIN KAEPERNICK
The Symbol versus the Shield versus the US versus Us

It was more than a year ago that he took the settlement. It was on a Friday, a perfectly picked Friday: the day after Valentine's Day, when all attention in sports for black folk was centered on the "Black Super Bowl," that is, the beginning of NBA All-Star weekend 2019. The "shield" kept it low key. No uproar, no public drama, no media victory lap, no major press release. Not even a tweet from Trump. The news just kind of broke in a "Yo, did you hear Kaepernick and the NFL settled?" type of way. Brilliant. By Monday—President's Day, in fact—people were in their feelings about the settlement. *All* in.

The Undefeated's platform ran the gamut: "Colin Kaepernick Won. Period." by Jason Reid; "Colin Kaepernick Doesn't Need The NFL To Continue His Fight" by Martenzie Johnson; "Did Kaepernick Sell Out His Legacy to the NFL?" by William C. Rhoden; "Kaepernick Sacrificed His Career—What More Do People Want?" by Bomani Jones. Jemele Hill waxed poetic justice in the *Atlantic*: "Kaepernick Won. The NFL

Lost." Jonathan Jones did the same in *Sports Illustrated*: "The Kaepernick Settlement: Why Measuring Victory Has Nothing to Do with a Dollar Amount." All making quiet statements about both the outcome and the future of possibly the most important black sports story of this century. All feeling the same way—not really knowing what to feel.

It felt like an unjust war had just ended without knowing who really won. There was a strong "So… *this is it?*" feeling for so many of us who for the past three years had attached ourselves both to Kaepernick's story and his cause. The emotion was stranded somewhere between victory and sellout.

Before we get to the aftermath, there needs to be a reminder.

Kaepernick: the son of a bitch among a league full of sons of bitches. The reason the NFL's ratings dropped in 2016, the reason NFL interest *and ratings* dropped in 2017; the reason "poor leadership" in the NFL became a reality. This, according to the president of the United States, news media reports, information released by the NFL, and the president of Papa John's Pizza.

GQ's Citizen of the Year 2017 cover. *Sports Illustrated*'s 2017 Muhammad Ali Legacy Award recipient. Jay-Z rocking his jersey in a *Saturday Night Live* performance. Erykah Badu taking a knee, announcing, "This is for Kaep," while hosting the 2018 Soul Train Awards. Love from Kendrick Lamar during a Forbes summit: "[He] wants to stand for something. Simple as that. You don't look at the moment, whether it's gonna work or not. No, you look at what the next generation is gonna receive from it." A yourrightscamp Instagram account that has become a universal source of "Be Like Kaep" inspiration.

Then came the thirtieth anniversary of "Just Do It." Nike's "Dream Crazy" campaign, where they led the entire messaging with Kaep's face beneath these words: "Believe in something. Even if it means sacrificing everything." The apocalypse.

He is an affliction, if we are keeping it 200. A polarization inside a lightning rod inside an enigma inside an activist. A passive-aggressive living martyr. A militant in Nike clothing. An unemployed NFL quarterback who has inspired a movement by not throwing a football. Over the course of two years Colin Kaepernick became the most interesting *citizen* in the world.

I emphasize *citizen* because it openly implies that Kaepernick is unemployed. That he is no longer a football player, an active participant in the NFL. Which is very important to this current Kaepernick narrative. A reminder of the thought that GQ put into distinguishing him in their "Men of the Year" selections. *What do we call him? How do we identify him?* All of that went into consideration.

Many applauded the GQ recognition. Playwright Luna Malbroux gave the mag love, saying the acknowledgment was "well deserved." Others, like sports reporter Britt McHenry, lost all respect for the mag, calling its selection of Kaep "a joke."

The separation of praise and problems. What Kaep was—excuse me, IS—trying to tell America is that to us, to black people, the police are no different from the emboldened white people who have taken center stage since Trump's election. The only difference is that the police have killed more of us and legally gotten away with it.

A random scroll on Kaep's Twitter feed, the day after he was awarded the Ali Award from *Sports Illustrated*, shows the range from love to hate, respect to contempt:

Liberty&Justice 4ALL
  @diab_tyseer
  Dec 5
  God bless you, you're a true American-hero, speaking up for the innocent victims and injustices towards our fellow Americans,

If anyone doesn't see that, they're totally blind and soul-less . . .

A-Nese-ssary Good
@A_Nese_ssary
Dec 6
Congratulations Kaep, well deserved. Thank you for so passionately bringing attention to the issues of inequality and injustice and amplifying the voices of the long silenced.

Govfella
@govfella
Dec 6
This is absurd. That's ok though. This fake outrage and constant bashing of America is why Donald Trump won in 2016 and will win again in 2018 and 2020. Kaepernick is a punk.

GeauxVols
@kwessner1
Dec 6
Sorry that America offered the opportunity to a black man to make millions playing a game. Such oppression. . . .

Kaepernick's ubiquitous impact is well summed up in an interview with Kevin Durant in the San Jose *Mercury News* in November 2017:

> [He] definitely put me in a different place… He brought something out of people that they'd been hiding for a long, long time that needed to be revealed. I'd rather you tell me that you don't like me because of my skin than hide that [stuff]. So he kind of touched a nerve and the outrage from it made me a fan of him just because he decided to take all that on, but also tell a message of, "Yo man. Just treat us fair, treat us equal, we're people too. We're not less than you because we don't look like you."

"If they take football away . . . I know that I stood
for what is right."
— **Colin Kaepernick** to the NFL Network, August 2016

And they did. When the San Francisco 49ers quarterback chose
not to "participate correctly" during the national anthem as
it was being played prior to three 2016 NFL preseason games
(two out of uniform, one in), he was a part of a quiet storm that
turned into a very disruptive one. The black QB, whose prom-
inence had been supplanted by Russell Wilson and Cam Newton since he'd led the Niners to the Super Bowl in 2013, simply
decided not to stand during the anthem. A passive move, with
subtle aggressive overtones, it was a personal choice of Kaepernick's not to openly honor a flag representing a country that had
allowed the killing of unarmed black folks by law enforcement
to get out of control. (Well, more outta control than usual.)
Kaepernick simply wanted to be a part of the dialogue without
actually saying anything. Things didn't work out quite that way.

"I do not respect Colin Kaepernick's actions—I think
he is wrong in the extreme. And I think his frame
of reference about his own country is scant: S-C-A-
N-T. And I think that is stupid: S-T-U-P-I-D."
— **Bill O'Reilly**, to anyone who was listening,
on *The O'Reilly Factor*

Here's what so often has gotten lost in the Kaepernick coverage: He didn't start this. The media did. Specifically, writers
Steve Wyche and Mike Garafolo of the NFL Network.
　　Kaepernick had quietly, without any form of grandstanding
or seeking public attention, stayed seated during the playing of
the national anthem prior to the 49ers' preseason games for a
couple of weeks. Garafolo tipped off Wyche that Kaep was sit-

ting during the anthem and that he'd sat the entire preseason, and Wyche went to Colin and asked him why he wasn't standing. Colin simply refused to run away from the question. That's it. He didn't ask for any of this; he didn't seek any of this out. He simply did not back down from a question. He did the opposite of what America was hating Marshawn Lynch for. Next thing we know, Colin is Gen-Next's Rosa Parks.

White folks' new. . . . bi-nigga. Bye, nigger.

This paradox crossed imaginary broadcast boundary lines when ABC (citing "creative differences" with *Black-ish* show creator Kenya Barris) refused to air an episode on the topic of athletes kneeling, yet the network found a way to resurrect and reboot *Roseanne*, with Trump supporting as a central "creative" premise.

The angst and anger of white America toward Kaepernick was summed up by Lowell Cohn in an August 2016 piece for the Santa Rosa *Press Democrat*:

> Kaepernick has benefited from our miserable, rotten society—the one he says fails so many people. Who has benefited more than Kaepernick?
>
> He is a biracial young man who was adopted by white parents and grew up middle class in Turlock. He has been famous a long time. He is earning about $12 million this season and his skills hardly warrant that. He lives a privileged life.
>
> It's hypocritical to dump on a society that made you a prince, especially when you happily accepted that. It's strange to fight for the downtrodden while you live like that prince. Kaepernick has not thought out the obvious contradictions in his position. The mark of a young man not fully formed.

Cohn added in another column, "Kaepernick is all about fame and stardom and appearance and hype. At this point in his career, he is an illusion. If he doesn't get his act together, his career will be an illusion."

And it was.

An illusion that over the course of a two-season span turned into something no one saw coming.

In September 2016, according to many media sources, beginning with ESPN's Darren Rovell, an e-poll research survey gave numbers to the divide. Among African Americans, 42 percent said that they like Kaepernick "a lot," while only 2 percent dislike him "a lot"; 37 percent of white respondents said they dislike the 49ers quarterback "a lot," 51 percent said they "dislike" him, while 5 percent like him "a lot." (That's 88 percent total "dislike" from white America.)

Among white people, the split before and after the protest was made public went like this: 13 to 5 percent "like a lot"; 12 to 51 percent "dislike"; 7 to 37 percent "dislike a lot." (The poll also found that NFL fans' before/after split of "dislike" for Kaepernick was 6 to 36 percent; the general public's "dislike a lot" went from 15 to 42 percent. In a 2018 poll commissioned by theundefeated.com, two years after the protests began, the racial lines between favorable and unfavorable still stood: 80 percent of African-American NFL fans' view of Kaepernick was "favorable" while only 36 percent of white NFL fans shared the same view.)

These data can easily be used as a basis for validating that race in America goes so much deeper than just color. And the stark polarization of the numbers indicates how differently we see, view, and feel about race-based issues such as the anthem protests, as well as what black and white Americans fundamentally want to believe and take pride in.

Also making this white America's new biggest fear: Kaepernick's getting an opportunity to play in the NFL again and playing well. Which the NFL made damn sure didn't happen. At least not in 2017.

And here are the reasons (based on numbers) Colin Kaepernick should have been playing football:

- A quarterback rating (QBR) of 49.5, tied for twenty-first in the NFL (2016); twenty-third in adjusted net yards per attempt (ANY/A), ahead of Cam Newton and Eli Manning

- Sixteen touchdowns, four interceptions (2016)

- He was the only quarterback in the NFL with a negative passer rating in points added category, and the 49ers went from having the fifth worst record in 2015 to the second worst record in 2016 (4–20 in last 24 starts; 27.5 points per game in those starts), but Kaep was the only starting QB from 2016 who (outside of retirement or injury) wasn't on any NFL team's roster in 2017.

- An overall Approximate Value (AV) of 145. Notable players below Kaepernick: Larry Fitzgerald 137; Michael Bennett 131; Joe Flacco 138; Carson Wentz 125; Eli Manning 149; Trevor Siemian 155; Golden Tate 157; Dez Bryant 173; Michael Crabtree 176; Jimmy Graham 182; John Pierre Paul 200. All were active in the NFL in the 2017 season.

And Wentz, prior to his season-ending injury, was the front-runner for 2017 MVP, leading the Philadelphia Eagles to an NFC-topping 11-2 record. So why was he, as a QB with a lower AV rating than Kaepernick, afforded the opportunity and the benefit of an NFL contract and Kaep wasn't? Further comparables: Wentz was equal to Kaep in passing TDs (16) and rushing TDs (2), threw for more yards than Kaepernick in 2016 (3,782 yards to 2,241 yards), and had more attempts (607 to 331) with a 62.4 to 59.2 percent accuracy advantage, but was lower/worse than Kaep in average yards per completion (6.2 to 6.8), interceptions (14 to 4), fumbles (14 to 9), total rushing yards (150 to 468), and total QBR (79.3 to 90.7).

The Minnesota Vikings even gave Case Keenum, a quarterback only one year younger than Kaep, with a 43.4 QBR in

2016 and a career AV of 24, an opportunity in April 2017 to open the 2017 season, signing him to a single-season, $2 million contract to be the backup-backup QB for Sam Bradford and Teddy Bridgewater while Bridgewater was on the "physically unable to perform" list. Just imagine if the Vikings had taken the "only holding the numbers against him approach" with Keenum, as the owners claim to have done with Kaep? Just imagine how differently their season would have turned out.

The answer is hidden in Kaep's unemployment.

It is not just because of those stats that Kaepernick should still be in the NFL but also because *no one was forced to answer during the 2017 season for his not being in the League* with those stats.

Add insult to injustice. In 2017, the Seahawks signed Austin Davis: 36.7 QBR, 1 touchdown/3 interceptions with Cleveland in 2016; the Ravens signed Josh Woodrum, no NFL experience, dropped from blocking back practice squad in May (David Olsen, the guy the Ravens chose over Kaep, was waived by the team three days after they signed him); the Lions have two backup QBs (Jake Rudock and Brad Kaaya) who have never taken an NFL snap.

Reworded: *the twenty-third-overall-rated starting QB in the NFL in 2016, who ended the season uninjured at the age of twenty-nine, dropped—for some unspoken reasons known only to owners, team presidents, and GMs—to a totally unserviceable QB for all thirty-two teams in 2017.*

Blackballed Matters, too.

There's more detailed metrics from a November 26, 2017 *Washington Post* report, comparing Kaepernick's 2016 performance as QB to the 2017 performance of each team's most recent starter, using a stat called adjusted net yards per attempt (ANY/A). Among starting quarterbacks going into Week 12, ten were considered worse than Kaepernick, nine about the same (plus or minus 0.35 ANY/A), and thirteen better. And that stat only speaks to his overall performance versus starting QBs. Funny that we are talking about a man getting in the NFL at all, filling one of approximately ninety-four QB slots, yet his exclusion is being judged against only the top third of quarterbacks that start.

It's all bullshit. But bullshit that has meaning. Bullshit that made Kaepernick and his legal team bring "collusion" to the forefront, in the form of a grievance filed against the NFL. A case that will be hard to prove, but as the *Atlantic* admitted, it's one the "NFL was making *for* him" by the fact that no team was signing Kaepernick. Yet, right before the beginning of the 2018 NFL season an arbitrator denied the NFL's request for a summary judgment on Kaep's grievance in a motion that forced the case to move forward to a possible "trial-like" hearing.

Years from now we'll have to argue whether for Kaepernick—simply from a football perspective—it was all worth it. Player and activist Michael Bennett tried to bring the issue back to the forefront before the NFL players sat down with owners in that October 2017 meeting:

> I think the first step to even being able to even have a conversation is making sure that Colin Kaepernick gets an opportunity to play in the NFL. I think before we even negotiate anything about whether we sit, whether we stand [during the national anthem], it should be a negotiation about opening up the doors for Colin Kaepernick and giving him an opportunity again, because I feel like through everything, that's been lost. All of us are having an opportunity to be able to speak to our employers, but to think about the guy who started everything not to be able to have a voice at this moment, it just doesn't seem very right to me.

Of course, nothing close to that happened. Because, regardless of how many ways we want to dissect it, the NFL used Kaepernick to make a statement the same way they felt Kaep was using them to make his statement.

"No Country for Colin Kaepernick" is how the *Atlantic* put it, subtitling its feature before the 2017 season started, "It's very possible that the activist-athlete will never take another snap in the NFL" deck. Or, as Jerry Brewer prophetically wrote in August 2017 in his preseason column, "Sorry for the inconvenience fans, but black athlete activism is multiplying," in the *Washington Post*: "While Kaepernick wasn't even the first in this wave of athlete activists to take a stand, his methods were the strongest and boldest, and it has made him the enduring symbol of this movement. He has sacrificed the most; his NFL career may be over at 29." And if nothing else proved Brewer's belief to be fact, it was the NFL's failed attempt at getting Kaepernick to return to the league on its terms. Once Kaepernick and his team "hijacked" what they (and many others) felt was an insincere, staged, one-sided, individual workout in November 2019, the chances that Kaep would ever play in the NFL again were basically over. The controversy surrounding the workout only worsened his chances, widened the divide between both sources and followers. His no-show was the descending of an NFL coffin. His "power move," his rise.

It's going to be hard to hold Kaepernick up when we look back at our current political landscape, current political climate, and current political administration. The "not voting" stance he took during the 2016 presidential election may not have directly resulted in Trump's winning the White House, but Kaepernick's apathy, sentiment, and total removal from the voting process in what may have been the most pivotal presidential election in the history of America cannot, will not, and should not be overlooked. His visibility, chosen or not, meant that Kaepernick needed to be made aware of the ramifications of his every action or, more important, inaction. As *Boardwalk Empire* so eloquently told us: "You can't be half a gangster." The same applies to activism in the face of national political tyranny and electoral bigotry in a country that, as Kaep knows more than most, has a historical track record of electing narcissistic white nationalists into power. Not that Kaep in any way entered his "stance" with an eye on making a political statement or even getting into the conversation of politics, but when in a fight in America has everything to do with race and will have *direct* impact on the people you are protesting for, then abstaining from the political process at that time is unacceptable. Even for newly anointed heroes. It is something Kaep should have to answer for as long as he pushes himself and his activism on the frontline of American consciousness.

In a discussion with my wife and son, I asked my wife, who was "not happy" about actor and activist Jesse Washington choosing to date a white woman, if she thought that or not voting was worse. She without a bat of an eyelash said, "Not voting."

Colin Kaepernick said from the very beginning that he was not looking for approval, nor were his actions going to be something he was "going to run by anybody." As he put it, someone needed to "stand up" (funny choice of words) for people who are oppressed. And one of the ways he felt positioned to do that was by not standing during the arranged time on his job when America chooses at every professional sporting event to celebrate "America" in song: a song written about and for an America that did not regard people of Kaepernick's color as complete human beings at the time it was penned; written by an American who, in 1812, used the terms "land of the free" and "slave" in the same verse.

IJS.

America is what it is and will continue to be whatever the hell it's gonna be, whether NFL players—or Colin Kaepernick, solo—honors the nation's anthem in a way that America sees

COLIN KAEPERNICK   65

fit. Divided we will always stand. United is often something America forces us to stand against.

> "We pledge allegiance
> All our lives
> To the colors
> Red blue and white
> But we all must be given
> The liberty that we defend
> For with justice not for all men
> History will repeat again
> It's time we learned
> This world was made for all men."
> —**Stevie Wonder**, "Black Man"

I've said this often but written it only once: Power and privilege never surrenders an apology. Not even when cases of wrongful death pile up. Not even when there's video evidence that in America black life doesn't matter. Black people have been in a crisis with police for a long time. Damn near since there was a co-existence of an "us" and a "them," forced to share space and circumstance.

But that doesn't mean we can't coexist with one another or function as a nation-as-one. It just means that until this country comes face to face with what it is and with the flaws built into its foundation, being "as one" as a "people" is something that will never happen.

America kills. It kills those we don't like, it kills what we fear, it kills those we oppose, it kills those who oppose us, it kills itself. Figuratively and literally.

And while this may be the issue Kaepernick wants to bring to light, one that embodies the "us and them" conundrum, raising awareness of the unjust murders of so many black (and brown) people in America at the hands of police officers (and the acquittals that so often follow) will not end the societal, generational, and racial divide. The systemic differences in our existence and purpose won't allow it. Even with Kaepernick's silent screams. Even as the world watches.

The aftermath. Post-settlement. Kaepernick Anno Domini. Hate to say this out loud, but this whole thing is much bigger than Colin Kaepernick. And unless he becomes an actual martyr in the midst of this (not a living martyr who *appropriately* shows up to depositions in his legal battle against the NFL owners and executives in a KUNTA KINTE T-shirt, or one who settles for millions only to come back to playing football in the NFL and stand while the anthem is being played) then his fight—at least in this country, at this time—will not change a damn thing.

How does Kaep wash the white paint off him?

Bomani Jones may have said it best in his post-settlement commentary for the *Undefeated*: "Kap is Neo in this matrix, but he didn't answer a call. In a watershed year in American history, a personal choice suddenly belonged to the world, molded to fit agenda both noble and sinister." And the words of Chinua Achebe ring factual and render hope: "One of the truest tests of integrity is its blunt refusal to be compromised."

For Kaepernick the true test, moving forward, will be his power to do just that: To sustain. Stay woke. Ten toes down. Grounded. Rooted in the cause, married to his cause. Staying both on message and true to the message at the same time without allowing the outside world—that is, America or the NFL—to break him.

Advice: Remain resolute. Always. Keep choosing principle over profession.

As it is said in church: "God will hear a famous cry."

CHAPTER 5

BALL OR FALL
The Re-Characterization of LaVar Ball

"Let me tell you the story of Right Hand, Left Hand. It's a tale of good and evil. Hate: it was with this hand that Cain iced his brother. Love: these five fingers, they go straight to the soul of man. The right hand: the hand of love. The story of life is this: static. One hand is always fighting the other hand, and the left hand is kicking much ass. I mean, it looks like the right hand, Love, is finished. But hold on, stop the presses, the right hand is coming back. Yeah, he got the left hand on the ropes, now, that's right. Yeah, boom, it's a devastating right and Hate is hurt, he's down. Ooh! Ooh! Left-Hand Hate KO'd by Love. If I love you, I love you. But if I hate you ..."
—**Radio Raheem,** *Do the Right Thing*

LaVar: Scoop, you know why I painted my house white?

Me: Naw, man. Why?

LaVar: Because I said if the president can live in a white house, why can't I?

Truth is, we've all known LaVar Ball long before he entered into our lives. We all have a family member that's him. A cousin, a brother, an uncle, a distant relative we only see once a year but wish it was every three years. A best friend, a coworker, a local bartender legendary in the neighborhood for the stories he tells and the lies that somehow become truth. An ex-boyfriend, a former AAU or high school coach, an old college roommate you tell your kids epic stories about, which they believe you are making up... until they meet him.

He's the black Frank Gallagher without the substance abuse, Walter White without the Heisenberg DNA. He's Donald Trump without the power, inherited white privilege, or *Forbes* listings. He's Kanye West without the musical genius or entitlement. The bald Don King. He's two Don Cheadle characters, Petey Green and Mouse, but with an intact family. He's Richard Williams and Earl Woods, James Evans and Lucius Lyon. He's someone Dave Chapelle wishes he'd invented.

He's the negro we love to hate, the nigga we love, the brotha setting us back, and the father so many black men wish we had.

As Muhammad Ali proclaimed: "I'm good-looking, clean-living, and I'm modest. I am so modest I can admit my own fault. My only fault is I don't realize how great I really am." The world can easily imagine LaVar Ball feeling the same way and saying the same thing. No third person.

There's an old Nikki Giovanni aphorism: "I am so hip, even my errors are correct." That's probably what LaVar Ball will end up having on his tombstone.

I met LaVar with the intent of humanizing him. It was March 2017, around the time he was making himself infamous and famous at the same time, becoming his own news item. ESPN decided to extend a video "look-in" originally intended for January into a feature story on the family.

LaVar was sound bite. Click bait. Soon he had his own tab on ESPN.com. He'd gone on WWE. Gone on Fox and dismissed Kristine Leahy. Personalized "Stay In Your Lane" as his own quasi-misogynistic catchphrase. Pulled his middle son, LiAngelo, out of UCLA after LiAngelo was arrested in China for stealing Louis Vuitton sunglasses with a couple of teammates; pulled his youngest out of Chino Hills High School once the new basketball coach publicly announced he wasn't going to run the team's offense through LaMelo. Before Lithuania became LaVar's residence, before he became caretaker for his wife, Tina, after she had a massive stroke, before the drop of his brand's $495 ZO2 shoe, before he and his eldest, Lonzo, became the center and centerpieces to the Los Angeles Lakers' season-long "reality" show, we sat down.

By actually spending time with him—instead of doing quick interviews with him or just sticking a mic in front of him—we felt we could get beyond the "character" he was making himself out to be and the media was directing him to become. We wanted the man who, at the time, had not pissed off all of America—just certain parts, sections, and segments of it.

There's a difference between a fool and a damn fool. LaVar got the former on lock. And he'd be the first to tell you that. The latter is one who causes and has the power to cause damage that rains collateral. So when the news broke in March 2019 that family friend and Big Baller Brand co-owner and business partner Alan Foster had "appropriated" $1.5 million for himself, it became real easy for people to feel that the damn fool in LaVar had it coming. Because a damn fool gets no sympathy, a damn fool gets little love, a damn fool gets what's coming to him or her, because in most people's minds a damn fool controls his or her own destiny and fate.

In the two days I spent with LaVar, working on a feature for SportsCenter we were doing on the family (Day 1 we recorded an hour-long podcast for ESPN radio and Day 2 we were at the Ball family home in Chino Hills), LaVar proved at the time that *a damn fool* was far from who he really was.

As the last question of the interview at his home I asked LaVar if there was one life lesson he would want all three of his sons to learn, just one that he and Tina wanted to instill in them that he hoped would stick more than anything, his response was simple—and at the same time said damn near everything about how he functions.

"Family first" was his response. He also spoke of respect and pain and dealing with what outside people say and think about you, but in the end for him it came down to family. For better or worse.

Unfortunately, the LaVar Ball from those two days is one nobody will ever really know or see. He won't allow it. Neither will we. Because he will continue to allow himself to be represented in snippets. In sound bites and YouTube clips. Punchlines and catchphrases. Loud, not pensive; in angst, not in control. And that has been the two-way street he's existed on since his public introduction. The love, the hate. Going both ways. Speed limit: 85 mph. And highway patrol? At Dunkin' Donuts.

Even with the family's Facebook series, *Ball in the Family*, the editing process and time constraints of producing a reality show don't allow for the full-on version of exactly who Lavar Ball is, as opposed to who *he* wants us to *think* he is and who *we* want him to *not* be.

This is a binary thing, in that Ball is not alone in creating his own villain. He has us, yes *us*—the media outlets who use Ball as a gift that keeps on giving—cosigning on this. Thing 1 *and* Thing 2. Him, us. Case, point: former NBA player and *NBARadio* host Eddie Johnson believes LaVar will "shut up when the Lakers are winning." Many people believe the opposite. On January 7, LaVar damn near proved both camps right, with his attempts to overshadow the 2018 College Football National Championship Game the following day with his comments (made from Lithuania) in an interview with ESPN's Jeff Goodman.

The slug line? "Luke [Walton, Lakers head coach] doesn't have control of the team no more." Of course, a mini-outrage ensued. One that almost equaled the public interest in the outcome of one of the best/most intriguing National Championship games ever played.

But that's LaVar. That's not going to change. As he said in that interview with Goodman, which was ignored by the media: "It might be a strong opinion, but it's *my* opinion." Emphasizing the "my" by putting his hand on his chest and not following it up with inside information from his son or anyone else on the Lakers.

But we, yes *we*—the media and the people we put content out to, calling it nourishment—swallow it and spit out the blame on Ball. Blaming the chef, knowing good and well the food is one-star yet still ordering it. Not that LaVar Ball is innocent, but we can't sit back and act like we aren't his sous chefs. He. We.

Chris Broussard, FOX Sports NBA analyst and cohost of *The Odd Couple With Chris Broussard and Rob Parker*, speaking to the pressure that "LaVar Being LaVar" puts on his 'Zo and how "we" don't help the matter: "I don't want to put all of the blame on his dad, I'm not saying this as a negative, it is what it is. His dad's bluster, his dad's braggadocio, his dad's antics put a target on Lonzo's back. And not just from players, not just from Patrick Beverly and guys that went at Lonzo, but *from the media and fans.*"

The most important part of Broussard's statement: "It is what it is." When it comes to LaVar, that pretty much sums up everything: him, his public persona, his relationship with his family, the protectiveness and love he has for them, his parenting techniques, his beliefs, the beliefs he has about his kids' potential and futures, his public comments, his responsibility to the race and culture, his actions once a camera or microphone is placed in front of him, his newfound celebrity. He is a man who lives by his own precepts. He is a man who lives at the intersection of polarization, personality, embarrassment, and entertainment. No more embarrassing than anyone on *The Real Housewives of Atlanta*, no more dangerous than Dennis Rodman in black and pop culture, no more a danger of setting black folk back than Kanye or Omarosa.

Yet his public life has become what Queen Elizabeth might term an "annus horribilis." Only to the outside world. To Ball, his public life is probably better than he ever imagined or scripted. The cameras and attention are to him what vibranium is to Wakandans. He feeds off of it, and it has the power to define him only because he has access to it. He'd call his public life "beautiful."

And it's harmless. Yes, harmless. Even with the internal scandal surrounding BBB and Lonzo publicly severing ties with the brand and distancing himself from his father for a short time, the activity around LaVar only impacts his inner circle. But it is *what he has come to symbolize* that is the problem.

He says, "It's just entertainment." But is it? Take what you will from LaVar Ball, but understand the truth is that the only real damage he can do is to himself and to his family. Damage that none of us should have any say over or feelings about. It's his life, those are *his* kids. End of story.

The reason Bill Nunn's Radio Raheem preach is at the top of this chapter is because it describes the love/hate struggle that has become LaVar Ball. Left hand, right hand. The tale of good and evil. Not good versus evil. LaVar Ball, over the course of two years, has been cast as both. Good and evil. Love and hate. The static—and, remember, static is the story of life—he's generated is both massive and insignificant. Given credence by those of us who feed into what we believe he represents, failing to accept that he really only represents a family and a brand.

Yeah, love knocks out hate in the end of that story. As it does in life. But the similarity between LaVar Ball's life and Radio Raheem's opus is that even in defeat, the hate never disappears.

POSTSCRIPT: Since I initially wrote this chapter, the LaVar Ball story has continued to spiral in and out of control. First, during the 2018 NBA Finals I was paired by ESPN with a producer who had his own LaVar Ball experience in Lithuania. He had stories. First-person stories. Up-close-and-personal stories. Confirmed stories. Proven stories. Stories of a different person than the LaVar I have portrayed in this chapter. Stories of calculated and dismissive behavior, of plots and plans, of inauthentic*ity* and egomaniac-*ism*. Stories with endings I couldn't defend.

From there, things went Ringling Brothers—the circus of pulling both LiAngelo and LaMelo out of school and dragging them to Birstonas, Lithuania, to ball for what ended up being a failed showcase (which led to the stories of celebrity belligerence from people who were there), and the *Ball in the Family* reality show that seemed to be at the center of his and his family's every move (from his launch of the JBA to 'Zo's targeted diss track at teammate Kyle Kuzma to the alleged brilliance of his "leaking" 'Zo's meniscus tear in order for his son to remain a Laker and not be traded) soon came to define LaVar and his family's mission.

Then, in June 2018, the *Washington Post* ran a story that depicted LaVar as a negligent, insensitive, and borderline cruel and abusive husband. Six months later, the Better Business Bureau gave Big Baller Brand a failing grade as a company. This was followed by rumors of a Federal Trade Commission investigation because more than two hundred customer complaints had been made against the brand. Three months after that, the whole Alan Foster embezzlement drama blew up in the family's face. And questions about LaVar's involvement in Foster's scheme became fair game. Then, 'Zo's trade exodus out of Los Angeles to New Orleans.

All not great looks. All problematic in making—or attempting to make—a final decision about who LaVar Ball is, and more important to society at large, what he represents. As of the release of this book, without the benefit of conducting another interview with him, LaVar Ball seems to have become one with the persona he created as well as one with what the media helped shape him into. The question remaining, especially as he tries to hold both his family and business together, is whether he has become one with *the person* all of this has turned him into, considering what it's cost him and his family? And while LaVar is still representative of only the Ball family and nothing more ("It's a family thing. It's for the family," he often says), he is quietly—for black America—becoming the bell that cannot be unrung. Giving "let freedom ring" a whole other meaning.

CHAPTER 6

THEIR EYES
WERE WATCHING A GOD
Our Miseducation
of LeBron James

"My greatness gets taken for granted."
—**LeBron James,** December 6, 2017

No one knows for sure if LeBron James ever actually said those words; together like that, in that order. No one is sure if he ever made that *exact* statement.

But the problem, one of many that keep getting piled on and attributed to LeBron, is that it is more than plausible to believe he did say those words. That at some point during whatever interview was being conducted with him at that time, those words—"My greatness gets taken for granted"—came out of LeBron James's mouth.

What LeBron did say, what was actually recorded, was this: "I think people have just grown accustomed of what I do and it gets taken for granted at times what I do because I do it so often and it's been a constant thing for so long… It's like, 'Oh,

75

that's what LeBron's supposed to do.' It looks easy, but it's not."

Here's the narrative: manufactured "LeBron hate" sells. Here's how narratives work (especially against those who strive to be global icons and are chasing ghosts of GOATs): Comments get turned into quotes, quotes get reduced to headlines, headlines are sold as bullet points, and bullet points become the bullets society and the media use against you.

It's an age-old, aged-out system that most public figures who push the boundaries of greatness have to deal with. In sports, more than in most other walks of public life, it comes with the agreement of stardom and gets worse with the elevation to superstardom. From Ali's "No Vietcong ever called me 'nigger'" to Jordan's "Republicans buy sneakers too," comments in sports are understood to be fair game.

But the difference between LeBron James and every other GOAT before him is that they didn't have to deal with it in this age of unfiltered and unregulated social media. So when it comes to the narrative that has become LeBron's life, the "noise" surrounding a simple comment like "My greatness gets taken for granted" is the perfect launching point for a true understanding of our miseducation of LeBron James and his misunderstanding of us.

LeBron James used to not have issues. The move to Los Angeles changed all that. Not making the playoffs the first year, finally underachieving, being at the center of the Anthony Davis initial trade disaster gave his haters, misanthropes, the media, and (if we are being honest) his teammates something legit to hate on, and they waged themselves against him en masse. That said, overall, as icons go, he's been remarkably issue free. Of course there have been some missteps, but given how his life has been scrutinized since he entered as the "I'm the next b-ball god" cypher in 2001, his career has been a remarkable exercise in

how not to self-sabotage greatness. Or at least the apprecia-
tion of greatness. There's no Tiger Woods Syndrome, no Pey-
ton Manning backlash, no Kobe Bryant scandals, no Cristiano
Ronaldo defrauds.

It is we who have issues. Issues with fame, notoriety, success,
attention, and attention-grabbing; issues with not being able
or allowed to construct and control someone *else's* narrative.
We, with LeBron James as the current and generational center
of the basketball—and sports—universe, have done our part in
casting both glory and shade upon him that will be unexplainable years from now. It won't even make sense. The problem
here is that James acts like we—our issues—don't exist. And
that's a serious misunderstanding in an unforgiving and unfor-
getting society, poaching for prey. Ours is a binary approach
to public acceptance and celebrity judgment. The court of
public opinion has been ambivalent about LeBron, about his
career, about his place in history. Because simply being the
most extraordinary basketball player the world has ever seen
was never enough. We demanded more, expected more. And
even though more is what LeBron James has given the world,
it has never been enough.

THE LBJ PROBLEM I

The Scrutiny That Comes with Global Iconic Fame after ESPN, the Internet, and Social Media Were Invented

Here's what's been held against LeBron: he was anointed before
he earned it; he quits, "checks out," and does not "will" wins;
the whining, the flopping, not finishing or not making the
"right decision" (shot) with games on the line; he's not selfish
enough when it comes to scoring; he's got "bitch" tendencies
(often exposed on social media, shade in interviews, never sat-

isfied, and so on); sometimes his numbers can be impactless; he can often come off as honest but inauthentic; he's pretentious; thin skin (very, very thin); the #lebronthehypocrite movement (a reaction that followed him after his comments about the NBA/China incident); the inherited sense of entitlement/arrogance/vanity/perceived privilege; the lack of public humility; and more. Comments like this—from former teammate Channing Frye in 2017: "LBJ only giving you 60 percent during the regular season"—don't help. They make people believe that he doesn't all of the time give his all to the game. The worst attribute that can be attached to any athlete. Just ask Shaq.

Most of these are beyond LeBron's control but some... he owns. Most of these are unfair but some... fair game. The problems become bigger in nature when LeBron acts like none of it fazes him. Like he is "above" all of it, which he should be, but it comes off as if he feels he's above all of *us*. When LeBron James exits and King James enters. And that's where things go for bad.

The shade LeBron throws and the shade thrown back at him by a broader public is legendary. Just look at how a simple Instagram meme of Arthur's clenched cartoon fist with "Mood" written beneath it, posted while the Cavs were struggling, not only created an internet firestorm at the time but came back to him months later, during the Golden State Warriors' championship parade, when Draymond Green revived LeBron's Arthur image on a T-shirt, but with championship rings: defibrillator.

Diminishing returns. Yet in the end, it all bleeds into how we witness and take in what LBJ does—*and does not do*—on the court.

On March 25, 2016, almost three months before the 2016 NBA Finals that would change LeBron's career, a post appeared on the site locker-report.com, titled "LeBron James: Stop Crying, Bro!" If nothing else, it captured the sentiment and consensus of the broader public feeling about LeBron in that moment.

All great leaders have a different approach. Tim Duncan is quiet and stoic . . . leading by example. Shaq was fun-loving but had an intimidating presence. Kobe is forceful and requires his teammates to get on his level or else. Jordan was a "killer," but he knew how to delegate when necessary. Magic had the ability to take over, but he preferred his teammates to be a part of the process.

LeBron is like Magic. He doesn't need all the credit for the team's achievements. He doesn't mind delegating and allowing others to take the lead. His approach is criticized, but it's effective. Five straight NBA Finals appearances confirm that it works.

Where LeBron fails, at times, is forgetting that he's 6'9, 270-pounds and the most gifted NBA player of all-time. He does have the ability to impose his will. Detroit in 2007 and San Antonio in 2013 are examples. His performance in last year's Finals: 35.8 points per game, 13.3 rebounds per game and 8.8 assist per game is another example.

The Cleveland Cavaliers came up short in that series. But it had nothing to do with James. They, as James opined, "ran out of talent." Kevin Love and Kyrie Irving, the Cavs second and third options, were sidelined with separate injuries.

Even with Irving and Love sidelined, James almost beat the Warriors going one on five. That's how great he is.

Irving and Love are healthy now, though. His team acquired a solid stretch big–Channing Frye. And, albeit controversial, the Cavs management fired David Blatt, a European import, and replaced him with a more competent Tyronn Lue.

Nothing is standing in the way of another NBA Finals appearance for James. The Eastern Conference is stronger (maybe stronger than the Western Conference for a change), but no team is strong enough to give the Cavs reasonable resistance.

I would never begrudge someone from wanting to reach another level, even if you're already at a high-level. There's still a way you go about it. And LeBron is going about it wrong.

Agree or disagree, agree to disagree, or just DGAF, a writer had just pretty much used a site's platform to spit an all-over-the-place referendum on how so many were seeing and feeling about LeBron. Of course, months later, that had changed. LeBron (with a healthy and hell-bent Irving) came through in a Game 7 classic and took the crown from the Warriors, putting much of the LeBron "hate" to bed. But not forever. Because as much as there were still moments—dissected with surgical precision due to the free-flowing recklessness of social media—where LeBron seemed to be on some GOAT requiem, his on-court, not-so-GOAT moments led a life of their own.

A Sample: Game 4 NBA finals 2017
(in Cleveland, Cavs down 2–1)
Score 84–83 (fourth quarter, ten minutes left on the clock)

- LBJ misses from twenty-five feet (9:11)

- LBJ turnover (7:56)

- LBJ layup blocked by Draymond (5:33)

- LBJ misses from twenty-five feet (4:43)

- LBJ: the Draymond incident (2:42)

- LBJ fouled; makes one of two freethrows (1:12) [96–89]

- LBJ scores six meaningless points in last forty-five seconds while Warriors keep a seven- to eleven-point lead. Cavs lose.

The takeaway: in a one-point game with ten minutes left, LeBron only took four shots in a seven-minute span. Two missed, one blocked, one fouled, and one turnover. Proof that in this LeBron era of professional sports when scrutiny rules, it takes more than just being great to be in the "greatest ever" conversation. Basically, the question is why should this global icon—who calls himself the King, as well as the GOAT—be uncomplicatedly revered? Dude shouldn't win even when he wins. That's that LeBron life.

The LBJ Problem II: Power

Danny Ainge, David Griffin, Dell Demps, R. C. Buford, Masai Ujiri, Bob Myers he is not. But he's been "publicly" considered a defacto GM ever since 1) he was targeted as the one demanding the Cavs trade Andrew Wiggins to get Kevin Love; 2) his partnering company, Klutch Sports, started fighting for Tristan Thompson to get what was then a max deal, so they could remain playing together in Cleveland. Then Klutch fought the same fight for J. R. Smith. And after both Thompson and Smith didn't consistently "earn their pay grade" (a term "insiders" like to throw around when discussing players they feel are overpaid) the sentiment continued to grow, as 3) his business partner Rich Paul, who heads Klutch Sports, told the New Orleans Pelicans that Anthony Davis was not going to re-sign with the Pelicans in a perceived power move (aka "the disaster" referenced earlier) to get Davis to play with LeBron in Los Angeles. From those actions, people looked at LeBron as the one who initiated and negotiated these deals. And he wasn't.

But like Solange, LBJ, in the minds of most, had a seat at the table. With that came, of course (insert sarcasm), the belief that LeBron got his former coach David Blatt fired. And ultimately somehow, LeBron will be the reason that his last coach in Cleveland, Ty Lue, was released by the Cavs, or gets another chance to head coach in the NBA; he will be the reason, eventually, that led to the ousting of Luke Walton in Los Angeles. Even though the Cavs fired the GM LeBron wanted to stay (Griffin) and traded Kyrie Irving despite LeBron's asking them not to, attributing more day-to-day power to LeBron than he actually possesses has been a problem since *before* he came into the NBA. Hell, when they moved the McDonald's All-American Game in 2003 from Madison Square Garden to Cleveland for him, that was the first indication.

LeBron James has always been seen as the elite sports power broker of this generation. And quiet as kept, especially with the $1 billion lifetime Nike deal he secured in 2015, he is. And he flexes it well. Almost perfectly. His vocal and active leadership in support of the SB 206 "Fair Pay to Play" Act, using the platform of his television show *The Shop* to get California's governor, Gavin Newsom, to officially sign the bill, was just one of the most recent. The coup he and Maverick Carter and their SpringHill Entertainment group scored with *Space Jam 2* and its extended portfolio alone speaks even deeper to the extent of his power index. But that has not stopped his power as a broker from haunting LeBron over the course of his basketball life. And when his teams—teams that, because of his open complaints over the years of not having enough, everyone *feels* aren't playing well—fail to win, he takes the hit for both the teams' performance and construction. As if his name is on the bottom of his teammates' checks. As if the franchise is really his kingdom.

Here's a small mock breakdown of the Cavs' 2016–17 core in the off-season and the "team" media sources kept saying LeBron wanted to keep intact. LeBron's "agency," Klutch Sports, run by business partner Rich Paul, handled the contracts of both Thompson and Smith and was negotiating at the time on their behalf.

2016–17 salary cap: $94.14 million; luxury tax: $113.3 million

Players LeBron wanted/fought for since returning to Cleveland:

Kevin Love: five years/$113 million ($21 million base), signed 2015

Tristan Thompson: five years/$82 million ($16 million base), signed in 2015

J. R. Smith: four years/$57 million ($13 million base), signed 2016

Iman Shumpert: four years/$40 million ($10 million base), signed 2015

Matthew Dellevadova*: four years/$38.5 million ($9.6 million base), signed and traded in 2016

(*Delly was signed as a restricted free agent to a four-year, $38.43 million deal, then immediately traded to the Milwaukee Bucks)

Not included, the remaining core:

Kyrie Irving: five years/$94 million ($18 million base)

LBJ: three years/$100 million ($30 million base)

If Delly had been added to the Cavs' 2016–17 roster, that would have been a total of $117.6 million for seven players with the pre-penalty luxury tax line set at $113.3 million. That would have put the Cavs already $4 million over the lux tax, with five more players to pay to fill out a roster. At the time of Thompson's signing in October just prior to the 2015–16 season, according to reports, the Cavs totaled $290 million of guaranteed money for just five of their seven core players. And that total didn't include the new contract increase Smith was looking for in 2016 or Irving's contract as the team's third-highest-paid player.

Keep in mind, the salary cap jump from $70 million to $94 million for each team was made official in July of 2016; from $94 million to $99 million entering the 2017 season. So the top-heaviness of the five players turned out to be not as egregious as originally perceived, but— in the court of public scrutiny—the damage had been done. And LeBron's genius as the team's defacto GM *straight publicly murdered.*

But not as badly as it was in 2019, with the pre-trading deadline move made to get Davis to the Lakers. The entire fallout was attached to LeBron because he has a share in the company representing Davis, and the Lakers was one of the only teams Davis claimed he wanted to play for and possibly re-sign with, once his contract was officially up in 2020. Optically—because he was so connected to both ends of the situation—LeBron found it impossible to distance himself. More than anything else that has happened to him, the Davis debacle confirmed people's belief in the power LeBron actually carries. And this may end up being the one that will follow him the longest.

The LBJ Problem III: The Debates

There are three debates that have haunted LeBron's career. Two he's been able to shake; one he'll probably never be able to escape.

The Kobe Debate is simple. Efficiency: that's the single separator. Not that efficiency—especially on the offensive end, when it comes to scoring—isn't important, but it didn't really became a "thing" until LeBron became the analytical movement's poster (man)child for how basketball will now and forever be played and appreciated. Their games differed. It comes down to a preference of style, not necessarily one of outcome.

Efficiency versus impact. Kobe's and LeBron's games, as well as their approaches to the game, are extensions of their personalities. They are who their games say they are. And while, over the years, this has proven to be more about personal preference than facts based on numbers, stats, or performance, there is somewhat of a misconception: LeBron has more clutch in him than he's actually been given credit for.

As Alex Heimann broke it down on Quora in May 2018:

> LeBron's teams were 16–6 in head-to-heads against Kobe; LeBron's points, rebounds, assists, and total field goal percentage averages were higher than Kobe's in head-to-head match-ups; LeBron's career "clutch factor" in major clutch categories including productiveness in the last five minutes of single-digit games and single-digit OT games and taking shots in the last five minutes of games to tie or take the lead, was actually higher and more efficient.
>
> The other side of that leans towards intangibles less concrete, but still essential to evaluating someone's greatness. Kobe was more fascinating to watch, which LEADS to appreciation; Kobe won championship after Shaq left LA with squads far worse than teams LeBron played on that didn't win championships (ie: Kobe won without Shaq, LeBron never won without Dwyane Wade or Kyrie Irving is the argument); and . . . Kobe had that "end of game killer character" that LeBron was never given credit for having—even when in reality, he did.

The Magic Debate is a little more difficult, for basketball purists. Everyone always speaks about the "completeness" of LeBron's game and how the real separator is his ability to do more offensively than anyone who's ever played the game. But in this argument, over the course of the last five to six years, someone either been forgotten or removed from the conversation: Magic Johnson. In the quest to get LeBron to Jordan status, Magic (basically) got shit on. Which forces us to ask:

When did LeBron just leapfrog over Magic in the "best ever" conversation? And after you answer the "when," ask the "why?"

As of the end of the 2017–18 season:

LeBron: 78 triple doubles (regular season), 23 (playoffs), 9 (Finals)

Magic: 138 triple doubles (regular season), 30 (playoffs), 8 (Finals)

LeBron: 4 MVPs, 3 championships, 3 Finals MVPs, 13 times All-NBA, 27.65 player efficiency rating (PER)

Magic: 3 MVPs, 5 championships, 3 Finals MVPs, 9 times All-NBA, 24.11 PER

LeBron: 1 scoring title, 0 other major single category titles

Magic: 0 scoring titles, 4 assist titles, 2 steal titles

LeBron: 10 losses of 30 points or more; 29 losses of 20 to 29 points (career)

Magic: 0 losses of 30 points or more; 7 losses of 20 to 29 points (career)

Funny, I put a Magic Debate in here when there really is none. At least not one in the general sports lexicon, but with their being so close in everything it seems fair for LeBron to be in a Magic Debate—and unfair to Magic that one doesn't exist.

At least not one discussed on *Undisputed* or *First Take.*

The Jordan Debate is extra. Everlasting, like the toe on Foamposites. In an interview with Hypebeast.com prior to the 2017 NBA Finals, the Jordan/GOAT question came up. Attached to it, of course, was LeBron James. My answer: simple.

> To automatically be in the Jordan conversation to me, I just think the argument to a certain extent is invalid because I've heard nobody speak about what's happening on the defensive end. The one thing that LeBron hasn't done is won Defensive Player of the Year. That's big, because if you look at the list of those that have won that award, none of them have been scoring champs. So when people say that LeBron is a more complete player, y'all are only talking about on the offensive end. It's like defense doesn't mean anything. With that being said, I want people to go look back at the voting of where LeBron has finished in voting for Defensive Player of the Year, particularly in his MVP years, and look at where Jordan ranked during his MVP years. That's a fair assessment because LeBron has never won it, but look at where he finished in voting in years he won the league MVP.
>
> There were very few times Michael finished out of the top five in Defensive Player of the Year voting. You start looking at that and you use that as a matrix of how we're going to judge these players. Yes, Jordan was a scorer, so LeBron's scoring isn't going to be there. Don't act like Jordan didn't rebound, but he's just not 6'8". He did get assists but he wasn't a playmaker like LeBron is. Don't just start making the comparisons between these two and leave out the defensive side, where I think LeBron is not even close. As great as he is defensively, he's not close to being as dangerous as Michael was. He doesn't have Michael's defensive acumen, and defense is 50 percent of the game.

Then I actually did the research.

The MJ versus LBJ defensive breakdown. In their primes. Ten years for Jordan, eleven years for LeBron. Eliminating the first two years of their careers because they weren't in DPOY (Defensive Player of the Year) voting at the time.

Defense:

MJ, 1987–1998: 1 DPOY; 7 times Top 5 voting, 10 times Top 10 voting, 0 times out of Top 10 voting

LBJ, 2006–2016: 0 DPOY; 4 times Top 5 voting, 6 times Top 10 voting, 5 times out of Top 10 voting (2 thirteenth place, 1 sixteenth place, 1 twenty-fourth place)

And, for added measure, MVP voting during that same period:

MJ, 1987–1998: 5 MVPs; 3 second-place finishes, 2 third place finishes

LBJ, 2006–2016: 4 MVPs; 2 second-place finishes, 3 third place finishes, 1 fourth, 1 fifth

Add to that Jordan's zero losses in the Finals to LeBron's six; add to that the fact that LeBron teams have been swept twice in the Finals and twice lost in five games; add to that the fact that not one of LBJ's teams are in the conversation of beating any of the legendary/all-time teams in NBA history. The latter is a major problem when it comes to a universal, heated, and for some reason personal debate that will ultimately be decided in bars, barbershops, bathrooms, and boardrooms by people who live for, prepare for, and will never let go of this argument.

Even the Harvard and Yale debate teams held a mock debate to confront this issue.

Just add the LBJ/MJ debate to the Biggie/Tupac, Federer/Nadal, Malcolm/Martin, Google/Yahoo, iPhone/Galaxy, *Washington Post*/*New York Times*, legalize/not legalize (weed), adidas/Nike, Godfather I/Godfather II, Frosted Flakes/Cinnamon Toast Crunch debates that consume our daily, weekly, and monthly cultural existence. Debates that will never be settled or, more important, resolved.

The LBJ Problem IV: Greatness . . . His Own

It has been held against him more than anything else. We may not hate greatness but we as a society *hate on* greatness. Especially when we are forced to discuss, debate, dissect, analyze, parse, compare, deconstruct, and destroy a particular someone's greatness directly against a particular someone else's greatest-ness.

And of all of James's "problems" this is the one that dives the deepest down the rabbit hole to become an obsession. *Has LeBron James lived up to or surpassed his own greatness?* It's the outside counter to the Jordan debate. When the reality is this: the fact that LeBron survived his greatness should be the only thesis. "The Chosen One" *Sports Illustrated* cover, the *SLAM* diaries, the ESPN nationally televised games, the initial shoe war to sign him, Throwbackgate, the Hummer, the celebrity, the *More Than a Game* documentary, media outlets documenting his life, the ROC Nation association, the $90 million Nike deal—all by the time he turned nineteen years old. He should have ended up as a cautionary tale of what happens when the world sets up a prodigy for failure. Instead, he survived, thrived, and still stands in front of us using his greatness against our weakness.

And in this post-baby boom-bap age of troll-centric information surfeit, that's a problem.

Here is when everything changed. LeBron doesn't know it, but the best thing ever to happen to him was Kyrie Irving's demand for a trade and the Cavs granting it. For the first time in the prime of his situation, LeBron could be judged on his individual ability in an attempt to win a championship. No real, first-ballot Hall-of-Fame help. Just him, the ball, the teammates, and the expectations. Which he exceeded.

In the 2017–2018 regular season and playoffs, LeBron almost unarguably had his greatest individual season of his career. A season that damn near ended the scrutiny—something most thought was impossible. And even though that whole "judging players in a team sport based on individual performances" is oxymoronic on so many levels, it is the law of the land in sports. LeBron is not immune to it, nor can he escape it. He gets no special treatment. No one does. Which is why he needed the 2017–18 season to happen the way that it did.

A season—especially the playoffs—that from a player/basketball/legacy standpoint was the best thing that ever happened *for* LeBron, though not necessarily *to* him. The Game 1 meltdown in the Finals after having *one of the greatest Finals games ever*, being swept by the Warriors, and the passive-aggressive "bad look" of victimization he attempted by coming to the post-Finals podium with a soft cast on his right hand (broken) almost damaged *all* the historic work he had done to elevate his legacy to new heights.

Victimized narcissism. It would have been a beautiful thing, except James might be the only super icon who couldn't pull it off. Not in this fake "Is Basketball More Important Than Your Dignity?" culture that follows around Kevin Durant but hasn't haunted James.

David French, senior writer for the *National Review*, authored a compelling piece preluding the 2018 Finals. In it he argued:

It's time to acknowledge that LeBron James is now the best basketball player who ever lived, the GOAT (Greatest of All Time). There is a certain class of basketball fan who scoffs at this notion. Fans my age and older vividly remember a singular night in June 1998. You know the moment. Michael Jordan slightly pushes off Utah Jazz forward Bryon Russell, rises up, and sinks the game-winning shot to secure his sixth title in six trips to the Finals. The instant the shot went in, I just knew that I was witnessing greatness. No one would be better. No one could be better. Until now.

Very, very, *very* hard to argue. Especially after witnessing (and *acknowledging*) what LeBron did in parts of the Finals that followed. But the argument didn't disappear. Because also on the eve of the 2018 NBA Finals, *USA Today* ran a story with this headline: "Now Is the Time to Have the LeBron James vs. Michael Jordan GOAT Debate."

Which coexisted on the same day that LeBron gave an exclusive interview to Rachel Nichols, answering the question about his comfort with his legacy, which aired on ESPN right before Game 1.

> Can I be comfortable? I'm never comfortable. I've gotten better with understanding that conversations are going to be conversations, no matter what. And it's so [pause] weird [pause] that people kind of categorize like individuality and then team and take away one individual and say, "OK, well, if you are *that good* then you should be able to beat *that team*." And I think a lot of that conversation [pause], that bothers me a little bit. But it is what it is.

And there it was. LeBron's mic drop. The comment LeBron James made that will not be held against him. Not like the one that opened this chapter. There's too much truth in it. Not enough ambiguity to make it mean something it doesn't. Instead (again, here's how narratives work), he's never going to stop hearing about that post-Finals hand cast, the timing and rationale for making it public, *and* the violins playing in the background like a scene from *Titanic*.

The confluence of factors weighs as heavily for and against LeBron as does the one-size-fits-one invisible crown he walks around wearing. He is a basketball god who has been built up and has also lived up to the hysteria that has too often seen him get in his own way. He has made it hard, sometimes impossible, to advocate for him: a superhero in a super-petty, super-sensitive, super-transparent world that feeds on assassinating superpeople's characters. As imperfect as LeBron is, the fault is not in his stars, it's in ours.

His career was never about belief or the ability to believe. His career continues to be—and always has been—about one man's contribution to the game, his place in it, and his being able to walk away saying that he gave his life to it. Which, of course, brings it back to Jordan. As everything does until someone new comes along. Until then, this "A God versus The God" paradox is what we are left with. Our Xenomorph, our Joker, our Killmonger, the monster-hero we created unnecessarily out of the greed to embrace debate and establish a generalized, GOAT-driven narrative.

And this might be the one area where LeBron can play the victim and win. Judging him against a Jordan that hindsight has re-created to be *perfect*, knowing that Jordan wasn't, is just wrong. Which forces us to hold up LeBron's incredible but imperfect career against a myth, ultimately judging him against a *perfection* that doesn't exist.

When it comes to King James that's not unfair, it's just fucked up.

POSTSCRIPT: The "legacy move" LeBron made by going to the Los Angeles Lakers has the chance to erase much of the public criticism held against him in this chapter—more than anything he's ever done in his career. *If* everything eventually unfolds correctly or close to perfection. Year 1 proved itself to be *so* not close to perfect. For the first time since he left Cleveland in 2010 LeBron did not end a season challenging for a ring. The pressure was off. But the "making the playoffs" pressure wasn't. Rather than an epic fail, the legacy move, for the first year, was an overall bad look for LeBron. Until the trade for Anthony Davis *actually* went through. Depending on what happens over the course of the remaining years of his LA bid, James's end could be very different from that of Kobe Bryant. LeBron's end game and how he ends playing *the* game are probably going to end up being two different things.

Like so many other things LeBron, both may change as the latest (final?) stage of his career changes. It's all fluid, all undetermined, all uncharted. But being a part of the Laker "family," whether he ever wins a title with them or not (especially after Magic Johnson's step-down as President of Basketball Ops and the Greek-tragedy-in-the-making drama surrounding the Lakers' front-office make-up and decision-making) will—more than likely—be a core experience in his basketball life that LeBron James will never regret making happen. Royalty welcomes him. History and his story indicate that LeBron'll figure it out before, or if, he signs another—his final—contract.

On July 9, 2018, the photo of LeBron with his agent Rich Paul and Lakers GM Rob Pelinka made it *very* evident: as great a basketball player as LeBron is—arguably one of the two greatest who've ever lived—for him, he's still a businessman and his life is still a business… man.

CHAPTER 7

BUOYANCY MATTERS

In sports, when it comes to power, positioning, racism, politics, and control, there are always situations that arise to put life in perspective. They act as reminders. As a journalist at ESPN, for me one of those moments came in the form of a story that involved a group of kids from the Philly area trying to go for a swim. It was a typical case of America exercising its boundaries. We. Them. They invite you in, then kick you out, *then* blame it on you. That's the m.o. Has been, will be; can't stop, won't stop. It's been repeated throughout black and poor people's experiences in America. Sports has not been exempt, on any level.

The following is a previously unpublished column I wrote in July 2009, when the incident occurred and became national news. The story had a short shelf life as part of the race-and-sports news cycle. Again, typical. No superstar sports figure name attached, no major sporting event surrounding it, no cameras on site to witness. Just a day-in-the-life (sports) story that—as they say in the industry—"didn't have any legs."

Color(ed) by Numbers

"Why are black people not good swimmers?
Because they don't have the buoyancy."
　　　　　　　　—Dodgers GM Al Campanis, 1987

As in any sport, it came down to a game of numbers.

"It was never our intention to offend anyone," Valley Swim Club president John Duesler said while standing outside the club that gained national attention last week with allegations of racism. "We severely underestimated the number of children and our capacity to handle these groups. We were not prepared for it. And that's the only reason [*sic*], it was a safety issue and that's the only reason that the children [*sic*], we felt it was not safe for them to be there."

How convenient. How true.

In an incident that involved the removal of African American and Latino kids from a swimming pool in a private suburban club surrounded by homes in the price range from $350,000 to $1.8 million, the belief was split along racial lines as to why, once the kids arrived at the pool, a white female club member (according to one of the kids asked to leave) was heard saying, "What are all of these black kids doing here? I'm scared they might do something to my child."

Sixty-five "black" kids in a 110,000-gallon pool seemed to be too much. Too much for the kids to return once a week for ninety minutes during the summer, as confirmed by a contractual agreement between the Valley Swim Club and the Creative Steps Day Camp of Northwest Philly.

Too much? Because after asking the kids to leave the pool and premises, the Valley Swim Club a few days later returned the day camp's $1,900 check with no explanation as to why.

Now, to many the incident was a misunderstanding. There

is no matter of race involved, it's a matter of numbers. As Duesler said, they "underestimated" the number of kids their facility could accommodate. It's a simple matter of bad mathematics. A misunderstanding.

How convenient. How true.

For the sake of racial harmony, let's say it was just a numbers mix-up. Then: 1) Has the person who made the mistake been disciplined? (Note: this same mistake, according to reports, was made with two other summer camps this summer alone); 2) Why wasn't the "mistake" explained in writing or by phone call with the return of the money to the camps?; 3) Why didn't Duesler say that initially, instead of telling two different local TV stations in Philly that the children "fundamentally changed the atmosphere" and "complexion" (*seriously?*) of the club?

This might help when it comes to the numbers: according to the 2000 census, the population of Huntingdon Valley is around twenty thousand residents. Of those, 19,312 are white. Only 153 happen to be black. The numbers representing the racial makeup of Huntingdon Valley lend deeper insight into why one side sees this as a misunderstanding and the other sees it as reality. And how the kids and staff of the Creative Steps Day Camp could come to (not "jump to") the conclusion that race played a large role in how their agreement with the club was not honored. Or respected.

Maybe when more than one-third of the entire black population of a community happened to show up at a private club it was a little overwhelming. Maybe it's safe to say that (judging strictly by the town's population) no one in Huntingdon Valley had ever seen that many black people together at once. Maybe it just took them by surprise. Any way you look at it, it's still about the numbers.

It's just coincidence that the kids happened to be black.

In the new multiracial, colorless, philosophical melting

pot America has (allegedly) become, things like this are no longer supposed to occur. We are supposed to be beyond that. Especially when it comes to sports and athletics. No one sees color anymore. The election of Barack Obama and the death of Michael Jackson brought us all together.

The convenient truth.

Which is why it was so easy for the president of the Valley Swim Club to hide behind the "numbers" game when attempting to give a reason why the Creative Steps day campers were asked to leave, even though they had paid for their time and both organizations had signed a contract.

Too many kids in a pool is dangerous. How true. Especially if the kids aren't the kind that people are used to seeing in pools. As wrong and politically incorrect as it might be, this problem could have been avoided by all us black folks simply embracing the Al Campanis philosophy, reading between the lines he drew more than two decades ago. *You people stick to basketball, baseball, football, and soccer.* Do that, and we (black people) can avoid problems like the Huntingdon Valley situation altogether, and won't have to worry about little black children being victims of such racial abuse. All we'd have to do is tell them, "No, they want you at their club, just not all at once."

More important, we would not have to live under the false impression that athletics—even as recreation—provide a safe haven of racial harmony and coexistence. Just as there are people in this country who still believe the color of our skin will come off in the water, there are still some who believe their kids will "get hurt" when "black kids" get in the pool.

And certain clubs want these people to be members and to remain members. Which is why some checks get returned while others get cashed.

So here we live. Waiting in the water. The Huntingdon Valley Swim Club is waiting for us to believe that it was about the

numbers; the director of Creative Steps, Althea Wright, is waiting for an official apology and honest explanation; the Pennsyl-
vania Human Relations Commission is waiting on the results of
their investigation; Senator Arlen Specter (D-PA), just waiting.

And a group of black and Hispanic kids are still waiting for
someone to explain to them what they should believe. Was it
about color? Was it about the numbers? Was it a combination
of both? The problem is, even when the kids get the answers to
those questions, they will still be absent of the truth.

Because just like bullshit, buoyancy happens.

POSTSCRIPT: In November 2009, Valley Swim Club filed
for bankruptcy and was sold in June 2010 for $1.46 million. In
August 2012, the justice department settled the racial discrimination case against the club for $1.1 million, which was to be
distributed among the seventy-three people—including coun-
selors—associated with Creative Steps Day Camp who were
directly affected by the incident.

While there was an excessive amount of sarcasm dripping
throughout the above column (probably the reason it didn't get
run), there should be no doubt about the intent, purpose, and
necessity of addressing the issue. At least from a journalist's van-
tage point. (Excuse me—a journalist with no buoyancy. See—
sarcasm.) Basically, this was "swimming while black" before
"swimming—or doing anything that involves the calling of the
police or law enforcement—while black" became a thing. Even
more now than when it happened, this incident represents just
a tiny sample of a much greater reality. A small part of a greater
story. Where, hopefully, the invisible line between the truth
and sarcasm will be understood and acknowledged. Even if
disagreed with.

And the truth is, this really isn't anything to laugh at or
about. No, it is not a major sports story but it serves as a familiar

sports narrative. An uncomfortable one. One that the people with the power to tell sports stories don't really want to have to deal with or be reminded of all the freakin' time. I get it. If I were them, I wouldn't either. And while sports has always been a catalyst to give us the groundwork (or excuse) to "hope for hope's sake" in America, this narrative will continue to be a reminder of the other side of hope. At some point soon, somewhere, sports will be at the center of a story (much like this one) that brings us back to the racial reality and hierarchy we live in, which we too often choose to ignore. The idea of the level playing field, where all things are fair and equal for everyone who participates in sports, becomes our sedative. Sprinkled over a nice craft cocktail to enhance the drink. Make it stronger. To f*** with our head. Only to make us face reality the next morning, wondering WTF we drank. And why.

Bruce Lee's philosophy was simple: Be water. Yeah, we tried that. Some kids tried to be one with it. It ain't working out. Time to be something else. Donald Glover musically and visually preached to us all: *This is America.* We need to heed that—and learn to stop expecting this America to be something it ain't. Or the next thing you know, some innocent kid will be forced into cutting his or her dreadlocks on site in order to participate in a high school sporting event, and we'll be acting all surprised and upset, screaming how racist and "un-American" that is. And we would never want something like that to happen, would we?

CHAPTER 8

FORMATION
An Interview with Jemele Hill

There used to be this running inside joke at ESPN between LZ Granderson, Jemele Hill, and myself. We gave each other nicknames, names that we felt people at the company might have been calling us, not necessarily behind our backs but when we weren't around. People in decision-making positions. LZ was Dr. King, Jemele was Malcolm X, and I was Crispus Attucks. Why him? Because I was the one they were waiting to shoot first. Metaphor.

Over the years Jemele has grown into more than a sports columnist. More than just a black female sports columnist. More than just a polarizing black female sports columnist whom the White House wanted fired. She is at at the forefront of a movement. A movement labeled "the intersection." A movement, to a degree, that this whole book is about.

Her professional candor and public openness have garnered her a level of respect most writers crave. And as her profile has risen, her voice and views have grown stronger. Which to many people in this country is a bad thing. After a buyout at ESPN she joined the *Atlantic*, bookending Ta-Nehisi Coates's long-form brilliance. She's the media's Beyoncé. All slay, every day. And by the way, as far as our careers at ESPN go, she got shot first. Martyr.

I had a list of three people I wanted to interview for this book: Hill, Michael Jordan, or Nike president Mark Parker. I chose her. Keep reading. You'll understand why.

Scoop Jackson: The space that you've been put in basically forced me to talk to you [laughs]. Seriously. The space we are in at this particular time with society and sports. From your point of view, what does being in the middle—at the center—of this moment feel like?

Jemele Hill: Well, I'm encouraged by the fact that it feels like so many more athletes, especially athletes of color, have become politically and socially activated, and that they want to be a part of this conversation. They want to be a part of the process. And that's great. But, the part that I look at very cautiously is, I think that they are still very much in the mindset of trying to do this in a way that is palatable for everybody. Not realizing that's not possible. Nobody is going to argue with somebody who is out there working in their communities, doing things through work. Those things are important. And I don't mean to belittle the idea of activism being your work but with that being said I think that [athletes] need to understand where voice becomes equally as powerful as work. It seems like they are still in the mindset of really trying to create movements and protest where nobody gets offended, nobody gets angry. You know? And I just don't even know if that's even possible? I mean that's not the root of a protest. So I feel like to some degree they are sacrificing their positioning, their influence, just to be nice to everybody.

And in terms of those that aren't athletes, I think fans are exercising more and more privilege in all of the wrong ways. And that there is this movement of people who, as I like to say, "Don't want their food touching on the plate." So they don't, they just look for the entertainment. Not that there's anything wrong with that, but I don't think they realize how much they tend to deny athletes their humanity by relegating them to props. [Their] response to athletes being more activated is disappointing. Because it feels like people have so quickly forgotten how sports can advance things in a way—in a very direct and progressive way—at a level that a lot of other sectors in society can't. People seem to have forgotten that part. Look, I understand it. I mean, we're in such a volatile and political time that people, because they feel traumatized by the real news that is happening every day, that they need these spaces of safety where they can go to and not have to think about it being bigger than what the moment calls for. But that's just not real life [*laughs*]. This "avoidance sports crowd" is interesting to me [*laughs*].

But don't you think some of that is on the athlete, that they don't really want anyone to feel "uncomfortable" with involvement in being outspoken?

It is.

Because fans can change their preference if the athlete comes out harder in the stances they take. Correct?

You know, that's an interesting way to look at it. I mean, I guess, I don't know if… this is like a chicken-and-egg thing… so, yeah, you are right, the fans would have no choice but to respond if the athlete doubles down and sinks into what they really believe, without fear of who isn't with them on the right side of history. And I guess what makes Colin Kaepernick's protest so special is that it's divisive in nature and in a way that, while it may not get everybody on board, it fully exposes a mentality and an attitude that a lot of people either wanted to ignore was there, didn't realize was there, or just missed. So there's even something to be said [for] the level of discomfort in anger for exposing what the actual problem is. And he's successfully done that. You know, as much as I am with the framework and the intention of, say, the Players Coalition by Malcolm Jenkins—they do a lot of "void work" in the community and they've certainly spoken up on issues—but they're still very partnership oriented. And maybe this is where I need to evolve, but in looking at every movement we've ever had that has yielded the kind of process that was necessary, it's always come painfully! It's never come because we up and decided that it was just the right thing to do. It's never come that way! So I am automatically leery of movements that are meant to be palatable for everyone.

I agree. And I think you and I share the same understanding in that, as black people in this country and knowing our history, that, hell, we had to fight just to drink water. It's as basic as that. So to come in "soft dancing," thinking that everything is going to be cool, that we can palatably do this without pushback or a fight, is not the way it functions for us. It'd be nice if change occurred that way, but for us there is no change without fight. Not in this country. None.

And never has been. So while players are definitely more politically activated, a little more socially aware, at the same time, I still think that they are very naive about a lot of things. What is amazing to me, and I look at college athletes in particular, is how they still don't realize the full breadth and scope of their power. Because today's black athlete is the most powerful that [they've] ever been in history. I remember I had this conversation with Tommie Smith—we were on a panel together—and I was struck because one of the things he talked about was how after they raised their fists, they came home to nothing. As in no jobs, no way of supporting themselves, no way of making a living. So everything they started by raising their fists, they couldn't keep going because they didn't have the financial means to do so. Now, you fast forward to today and a big reason why Colin Kaepernick's issues and why his stance are very much in the news is because financially he can keep it going. Like, he doesn't have to compromise because he doesn't need the money. Same with LeBron James. LeBron doesn't have to compromise. He can be on *The Shop* talking about a black power structure and how we need to keep things self-contained, and much more brazen topics and have brazen conversation about race, because no one can tell him what to do with his money! He has too much. And he's fully realized that part. That's why he can call the president "a bum." That's why. I think his peers and his colleagues don't realize that so many of them can do the same thing. And I think they get a little neutralized. While we all want a certain degree of unity, like, we all woulda liked to think that while Martin Luther King was fighting on the front lines it would have been easy to convince people that "Yes, we all should be drinking out of the same white folks' water fountains" or "No black passengers should be relegated to the back of the bus" or [that] some of the other conditions impacting black workers and people were unfair. We would have *loved* if everybody was on the same page about that but the fact is—they weren't. And as history has shown, during that time [King] was one of the most despised people in America. The majority of Americans were against protesting because they felt like it undermined equality. They didn't want the shit in their face. [*Laughs*]. It's that simple. They didn't want it in their face. And I don't know how much we've progressed out of that way of thinking.

True. But my only pushback on that would be to your point about how much power the athlete has is now rooted in the fact that he/she has money. I still have concerns that our power in this generation, if it's just connected to money, that limits us. It makes us chase something that we'll never have on the same level as other people in this country. It's why you don't see lateral movement across the board with the exception of people like LeBron, who does have the money and something to lose. I mean, once you add money to it, if money determines your power in this game, then we are still rendered powerless because we're never going to have that much money! Like Chris Rock said, "We might be rich, but they wealthy." [Laughs.] Who's willing to lose the money that they do have is what I'm concerned about, because that's what we don't see from athletes.

That's fair. It's the sacrifice part of it. It's sort of like we do want to serve two masters. And maybe that's just the way society is constructed, in a sense that we want power, we want more acknowledgement, we want more fairness, but to get the things that you want does ultimately have to come with you giving up something. And who is actually willing to do that?

That's what I'm saying! Exactly! Who's willing? Look at the history we are talking about and aligning today's athletes with: who had money? No one. Money was never at all connected to their activism. But you were given money or you made money, and that became the harness. That's what holds back your true activism. Because now you have something, now you are afraid to lose it.

Right. Right. Yeah, that's true. Once that becomes the kind of engine/driving force, it becomes that much harder to let go of and sacrifice. But, I guess though, there is that conversation, "Is it about money or is it about. . . ?" Like, there's a lot people who [could] not withstand what I'm sure is a degree of disdain—and I can see a lot of that disdain, honestly—and animosity toward Kaepernick. A lot of people can't handle that. So it's just not about loss of money, it's about the loss of what black athletes and black entertainers of any note have always craved: acceptance. And you're going to give up the acceptance if you continue to push back against the structures that have been [normal] to you for so long.

And that's a hard thing to do once you've been conditioned to believe that through sports your acceptance will only come if you do things a certain way.

Yeah. It's a heartbreaking thing when you see a lot of athletes kinda get hooked on that acceptance. And I get it. Because that was supposedly the end goal, that we would finally be accepted. Not just accepted, but accepted as equals. It's different. And when that doesn't necessarily happen, it can create...

'Nuff said. In your mind who has the most power in sports? Owners, organizations, players, fans, race, or gender? And I'm looking at each one as a group. It's a tough question to answer.

I got you. It is a tough question to answer, but I would at least narrow it to two answers because [even though] the players are the actual product—and this is where my argument for the owners comes in—most owners know that team is their hobby. That's not actually where they made their money. And because it's a hobby, they can treat it like [one]. So even though the player is the product, the player needs to make money. That's their livelihood. The business for owners is different. Sports and owning teams is not their main business, so what do they care. There's virtually no consequences for them in most instances in sports. And there's always a consequence for the player. Take the NFL, for example: look at somebody like Jerry Richardson [principal owner of the Carolina Panthers], who they essentially

ran out of the Panthers ownership because of sexual misconduct. He still got to sell his own team! He still walked away
with millions upon millions of dollars! So the only real consequence is, he doesn't get to play with his favorite toy. That's it.

You and I are so on the same page about that.

I mean, for most players once they stop playing... look, Colin
Kaepernick is only lucky in the sense that before he left, before
the football part of it was basically over, he had one big deal
on the way out, and that is what gave him a little bit of leverage and a little bit of comfort. But there's plenty of other cases
where that would not be the situation for everybody. As long as
the players exact their livelihood by playing, it's got to be the
owners that are the most powerful in sports.

Even above organizations like NCAA or, say, the NFL as a whole?

Well, the NCAA then, because that's made up of a collection
of schools. But if you want to put them as just owners, then
absolutely. And with the NFL, the organization *is* the owner.
The commissioner works *for* the owners, not the other way
around. They pay *his* salary. So even with that, it's still the
owners because they have so much sway and influence and
power within that organization that's made up of them.

*But they claim to acquiesce to the fans and say the fans hold the
power, but I've always believed the fans can only exercise their
power a certain way. I don't think they are as powerful as the owners,
organizations, or the players because they don't act collectively. Yet
we are told that we as fans have the power. And I think that's a lie.*

Yeah, I think that is a lie. You know part of having power,

though, is you gotta recognize that you have it [*laughs*] and the recognition on fans' part is very, very low, and they don't realize how much they are emotionally pimped when it comes to sports. They are! They are emotionally pimped. They are conditioned to believe in these organizations, and if you talk to any fan and you ask them why do they love a team or why they love a sport, it's an emotionally based reason 100 percent of the time! It is like, "Oh, I grew up watching this," or "Oh, my dad liked this team," "Oh, this…. Oh, that." They are too emotional. They don't have any power because they can't get control over their emotions and their emotional connections to sports.

Damn. Never thought of that.

Yeah. They can't stop watching football for something greater like supporting Colin Kaepernick or stop watching the NCAA because they don't financially compensate the athletes. And another reason why, and this you already know, when we talk about assessing, absorbing, protecting, and amassing power, division is the one thing that will undercut all of that. And because there's this "fans versus players" division, that's why the fans have no power. Because they don't understand that they have much more in common with an athlete than they do with an owner. Yet, they always side with owners. Always! They haven't made the correlation that the owner is. . . . You know that dude at your job, your supervisor that you can't stand? That's the owner! [*Laughs.*] They don't get that part of it. They don't understand that players are fighting for labor issues just like them. These are labor issues that all Americans have to fight for. Health care, all these things! But because of their innate jealousy toward players, they always side with the establishment. Again, always. So fans' emotions are being turned against them all the time.

That's a great point. One that I've often attached to the media and associated with access instead of emotion, but never related it to fans before. That's real. And speaking of media, I wanted to get at you about the media side of power as it relates to sports. Without getting too personal or political, I do want to ask you: Was Adrienne [LaFrance, editor of TheAtlantic.com] the first woman ever to hire you in your career?

Oooooouuuu…. Wow, let me think about this.

Was that the first time you've ever in your career in sports media been offered a job from another woman? Like shake hands, face to face?

Damn, you might actually be right. Damn. Like I'm really thinking and you might be right. I can't think of another woman who's had the final say on my position. Now I've obviously had women who were my bosses, but to be hired by a woman? No I don't think so. Wow, I think this may have been the first.

OK. What about a person of color?

Yes. Keith Clinkscales [former SVP at ESPN] was the only reason I got to ESPN. And then Lynn Hoppes [former editor at ESPN.com and former sports editor at the *Orlando Sentinel*]. Lynn was the one who brought me in.

So you've at least in your career had two people of color and one female offer you opportunities and you've been doing this how long?

Twenty…one… years.

You see where I'm going with this don't you? You never thought about that before have you?

No, I never did. And that's a good observation, man. Even now I'm sitting here asking myself, "Was I ever...? Naw, it was always..." [*laughs.*] That was always the case.

So I asked that to lead into this: In a piece they did on you in the New York Times, *you used the word "embarrassing" when you talked about being, at the time when you were with the* Orlando Sentinel, *the only black female sports columnist in America. I'm asking you, why did you feel embarrassed, knowing the state of the [media] game and knowing the country we live in, as opposed to just saying that your being the "only one" is "typical?"*

Well, first, I know that struck people as an interesting choice of words, but the reason I'm embarrassed is because I got into journalism for very emotional reasons. Meaning that, I wanted to be a part of something that was bigger than me, the pursuit of truth, I wanted to tell people's stories, and I wanted to be accurate and fair. When you commit from an emotional standpoint, what you committed to, what you want to think, your sacrifices, everything you put in it, is worth it, and at the end of the day it's to send things to a better place. And considering the variety of issues that we report on in sports, in media period, a variety of issues that have to deal with race, gender, we are the least equipped to do it because of what our own industry looks like! Yet, we've been put in charge of this amazing mission to make sense of stories and historical times with race and gender being a part of the discussion and we are the least trained, least equipped, least able to do it. And that is why it was embarrassing. We can't expect to be able to tell stories about multidimensional athletes when we only have one dimension represented in our business.

Do you expect change to come, or have you gotten to the point now, after twenty-one years, that you've gained an understanding and belief that before you leave this earth there essentially won't be that much change?

Well, I'll put it to you this way: in 2005, when I was the only black female sports columnist at a major daily newspaper in North America, I was one. Today, the latest statistic I've seen is that there's eleven women of color that are sports columnists in the country. All eleven are at ESPN. All eleven. So that would mean, just by definition, that at the daily newspapers there aren't any. To me, that says it all.

It's sad, more than embarrassing, to me. I remember [Michael] Wilbon told me something years ago, when I was at *Slam*, something that messed my head up. He said, "You right now might be the most powerful black sportswriter in America." And I was like, "How the hell you figure that?" He said, "Because you are the only one right now that can decide what goes on the cover of a national sports magazine." He said, "You are the only one in the country that has that power." It fucked my head up. I wasn't embarrassed, I was more mad, because that was the reality, and I knew, in all honesty, I had very minimal power at *Slam*. I had creative power, but not controlling power, you know what I mean? And here's the thing: that reality stands to this day and I'm not even in that position today. I've regressed in power. But the game hasn't changed.

Well, the thing is, you have to look at, once we start peeling back the layers, there's that first layer of "Are we even getting our foot in the door?" There's that layer. Then it's "What happens when we do get our foot in the door?" And that's a whole 'nother conversation. And there's just not that many of us in positions where we can decide content, where we decide what content to pursue, where we buy said content or decide where said content is placed. It's just not, there's just hardly any of us that are in that position. So with that being the case you can have like a pretty team picture all you want when it comes to diversity but the shit doesn't mean anything unless you've put empowered people of color in these kind of positions to make decisions and more importantly to be heard. You know. You don't have us in the room and we can't say shit? [Laughs.] That's pointless.

Exactly. And that's my whole thing is us trying to expect change is naive on our end. I think we can hope for change but to expect it is defeating. Like you said once: "The Obamas sometimes need to stop going high when people are coming at them low."

Right. [Laughs.] Right. You were on Don Lemon's show (on CNN) speaking about Jay-Z and ROC Nation's agreement/arrangement with the NFL. Continuing in the context of power and our lack of it in sports, can this move by Jay be looked at as strictly a power move on his behalf, or because of who he is and the lack of power in the game that "we" have, is it possible to look beyond the cultural—and racial—"slap in the face" his move seems to have been?

I'm struggling to understand what power Jay-Z actually attained. What seat at the table does he have now? Maybe it's something I'm just not smart enough to understand, because what I see thus far is that the NFL convinced him to leverage his vast and powerful relationships in entertainment to help them curate music for some of their biggest events, including the Super Bowl. It's no secret the NFL's Super Bowl half-time show was faltering. A number of black artists refused to do the show out of respect to Colin. That put the NFL and the artists who did perform in the show in an awkward position. The NFL doesn't want to answer questions about Colin Kaepernick during the Super Bowl. The league wants to be able to showcase the artists who perform. They don't want them questioned about Kaepernick, either.

I'm aware that Jay-Z will help them amplify their social justice initiatives and while I'm sure that will be worthwhile, there's also a ton of power in discomfort and awkwardness. Powerful entities like the NFL don't like to be questioned. It was necessary for the NFL to feel this awkward tension from the black community. Not to mention justified. The NFL's treatment of Colin Kaepernick had a lot of black folks questioning their loyalty to the NFL. A lot of black fans were flat-out turned off. During the Kaepernick fallout, it seemed as if the NFL only was interested in appeasing its white customers and Donald Trump. They didn't care that black players were deeply affected and traumatized by these brutal acts of police violence, or by the words and actions of a bigoted president. They didn't care that many black fans wanted the players to use their platform to bring awareness to these critical issues.

The NFL adopted a familiar mentality we've seen with outspoken black athletes, whose value is usually seen through the prism of the entertainment they can provide. That's why it felt the NFL was really weaponizing Jay-Z, instead of partnering with him.

And does this move by the NFL further dig a (black) hole for them because it seems so superficial and obvious what they are trying to gain from it?
The NFL got what it wanted, and a lot more. They certainly wanted to strengthen and, to some degree, reinvent their relationship with black culture and entertainment. But as an added bonus, Jay-Z now has to absorb the backlash that really should be directed at the NFL, because the NFL isn't the one answering questions about Colin Kaepernick. Jay-Z is.

So, not post-racial. It seems like the new sexy term being used is "At the intersection of sports and race and gender and politics and culture." It was used to launch The Undefeated, *it's being used to introduce you at the* Atlantic. *I would like to know from you—since you are at the center of it, you are in the crosshairs of it, like the new Public Enemy symbol of it—what does that "intersection" look like?*

[*Laughs.*] Well, for me it looks like honesty. And the unfortunate part is that although we have a lot of entities out there who want to cover these issues that we all agree have always been there, the problem is *it takes guts* to be able to do it. What happens is because so few people are willing to piss off people in the process, a lot of people don't have the guts to cover these intersections honestly. So if you want to talk about race and gender in sports, that means you have to talk about white supremacy and white privilege, and you have to talk about patriarchy, and you got to talk about toxic masculinity. But nobody wants to go there! They want to talk about it as a highlight, as a feature, and say, "Oh, isn't this great this barrier is broken?" But you don't want to talk about why that barrier was there in the *first place* and, most importantly, who put the barrier there to begin with and why? So that's why this work requires a level of honesty that I fear most do not have. And while it is kinda funny to me, like you, we've both been doing this work before it was called "an intersection" [*laughs.*], before they put that name on it, but you know I'll say that I noticed that there's a service-level treatment of these issues, because you can have that kind of meeting and you can make that an emphasis of coverage, but if all of the people deciding to cover it—or, for that matter, choosing what to focus on—if they all look like or are the establishment then you really ain't gaining that much ground. You're just covering intersections that white people can deal with. That's what you are doing.

We've been trying not to do that for a long time but it seems that's where we kinda get stuck or placed, and if we try to go too far outta that space we lose a lot of the shit—the work, the stature, the so-called titles, the respect, et cetera, we put ourselves in a position to have—and the power to make change. Does that make sense?

No, that makes total sense. To do this work of covering these intersections and, for that matter, talking candidly about race and sports, you have to realize that it's supposed to get a little messy. And I don't know that people are honestly equipped to handle the mess. They don't really know how to cover the mess, they don't want things to get messy. So therefore you end up doing that kind of work, our kind of work, a disservice because you are just covering it to say that you did, and that this is something you are committed to—when you're... really... kinda... not.

CHAPTER 9

ILLMATIC
The NCAA's Fraud Perfection
(A Novella)

A boy is born. In Hardtime, Mississippi.

Surrounded by a family not so pretty, a dollar and a dream. That dream? To be the next LeBron James, Baker Mayfield, or Hunter Greene. His Moms, still a teenager. Seventeen years younger than his grandmother. Got all his dad's features but not his last name. Kid's got big hands and feet for a newborn. The doctor notices. Labels the child before the umbilical cord is cut. "This kid's going to be an athlete" are the next words out of the doctor's mouth after he tells his patient that she has a boy. Predestined, predetermined, predicted.

The Mississippi life is no joke. Never has been. But for those that live it, it is what it is and it is what they make it. Jimmy Crowe (the kid's name, no relation to Russell) lives that life. Grade school prodigy, high school phenom. Every SEC school wants him, damn near every coach has been to his house. Rich white families want to adopt him, richer shoe companies want to sign him. Both know that's totally not possible, but it doesn't hurt either from getting to "know" him.

Jimmy has no blindside. Nothing surprises him, nothing sneaks up on him. He has a capacity to soak up knowledge that is opposite of the stereotype placed on athletes who come from where he does. At an early age Jimmy opened a book and he liked it. Still Jimmy only saw one way out. Again, he knew others existed, but he only *saw* one. He only heard one. No one redirected his path, the one in their minds that God had planned for him. Him *and* them.

His life and the lives of those around him reflect Nas's first-verse lyrics on "Echo," just without the NYQB backdrop. Black and bleak, not bad or bougie. But still fulfilled. Everything Jimmy has comes from inside. Heart, warmth, spirit, soul. A good place. His friends call him "Chidi." He's dropping twenty-nine points per game. His team is ranked number three in the nation. At six-feet-seven and 228 pounds, the Baby LeBron comparisons are regular.

On selection day, he squashes a Kentucky New Era over his oversized twisted textured 'fro. Coach Cal had gotten to him in a way none of the other coaches had. Told him things he not only believed but knew would come true. Things he knew *he* could make happen without people at the school claiming, once he became an NBA star, they'd made them—or allowed them to—happen for him. The Mississippi grind that was Jimmy's life outside of ball fostered a foundation of independence and severe self-sufficiency. To Jimmy, accepting a scholarship to play ball was a means to his endgame. He was taking advantage of them; they were taking advantage of him. One hand washes the other. Except they had more soap.

He wanted to keep it in the South, keep it close to home, to what he knew, to what he could control. Hardtime, Mississippi, remember, it never leaves one's bloodstream. Jimmy'd heard too many stories of ball players taking scholarships to play for schools that had no connection to who *they* were, and those players ending up being shaped and defined by the school they went to and played for as opposed to the other way around. In Jimmy's mind, he repped him and his. Nothing more. UK was just one of the spots on his life's journey. He never wanted his blood to turn blue. He liked the color it was. Matched the color he was on the outside.

State championship. McDonald's All-American. Jordan Classic. Nike Hoop Summit. Slam All-American. His team came in within two points of beating Findlay Prep (NV) and playing Montverde Academy (FL) in the GEICO High School National Championship finals. MaxPreps/247Sports number three–ranked player in the country. Another guaranteed one-and-done. Jimmy Crowe's future was on the fast track, if he just played *the game* correctly. And it was all good until Jimmy set foot on campus.

"Yo, JC, let's go grab something to eat from Tolly-Ho. My treat."

Brock was one of the non–basketball players that Jimmy kicked it with. They met in Introduction to Writing, Rhetoric, and Digital Studies. Shared the same inside joke about the instructor. Been tight ever since. Brock is from Los Angeles, at UK on an academic scholarship, full ride with benefits, studying Intercultural Communication through Media and Film in the College of Arts and Science.

It's the "my treat" that separates Brock and Jimmy. Not that their fams were different or that they came from different upbringings despite the geographical and societal contrasts that molded them. No. It was the simple fact that Brock was able to have a job while he was "being paid" to attend UK and by law Jimmy couldn't. That whole NCAA thing. The regulations, the restrictions. Although they'd both signed "agreements" to be students, there were things Brock could do that Jimmy was not allowed to do. Not without jeopardizing his scholarship, being in breach of contract, and putting the university's entire sports program under a Robert Mueller. "My treat" was their code. Code for the real, code for the bullshit of it all. Something they discussed all of the time.

"One day, I'ma treat," Jimmy said.

"Next year, once that NBA check is official," Brock joked back. "And we won't be eating at Tolly-Ho's either."

"It seems like that's how this whole thing is set up, fam. That because I have this opportunity, this *non-guaranteed opportunity* in front of me, I'm not allowed to function as a normal student or just a normal human being while I'm in school here. Pretty fucked up."

Brock replied, "You understand though that while I 'work for' University of Kentucky, you, my man, 'work for' the NCAA. There's a difference."

"Why?" Jimmy asked angrily. "Why is there a difference? We both students, both on scholarship, representing the same school. This is some bullshit."

And that bullshit is what's at the center of the pay-to-play argument that has haunted American college athletics for decades. An argument that has over the last five years taken on a life of its own. An argument that is rooted in economics, education, unfair labor practices, race, corruption, class, ethics, policy, and power. Jimmy, as a basketball player for school that generates $26 to $27 million a year from its basketball program, is both victim and product. His argument against the system he plays in and benefits from holds little weight outside of complaining with Brock, because he knew what he—and his family—were agreeing to when he signed his name on that Letter of Intent. All NCAA D1 scholarshipped athletes do.

"Dude, in high school for this paper I was doing for an econ class my junior year, I read that the NCAA was making like $700 million in royalties on retail sales of merch annually, it was a $13 billion, yo, billion-dollar-a-year business," Brock blurts out. "The fact that you gets none of that is foul. You getting an education bro but that $40G tuition ain't nothing compared to what they are making off you all."

Brock takes a sip of Pepsi. "That's new-school slavery, bro, if you ask me."

Jimmy refuses to take it that far. As his basketball season is set to begin, the NCAA has just unanimously voted to, in 2021, allow players to reap financial benefits from their names and likenesses and to profit from their being "campus stars" while still co-eds at those schools. Yet Jimmy is unaffected. He'll be in the NBA by the time that new rule comes into play. Again, as he tells himself daily, he signed up for this. Plus, being from the South, Jimmy has a much different connection to slavery than Brock does, being born and raised in LA. More than the money generated through athletics at UK that he is not getting a piece of, Jimmy's bigger beef with the NCAA's rules is how he, as a student-athlete, is not allowed to earn or receive any money in any form. How he can't get a job, how he can't do anything extracurricular to generate an income, how he can't borrow any money from coaches or teachers or any of the boosters who flaunt the money they are making off him in front of his face, to buy a train ticket back to Hardtimes for a visit or help him pay his iPhone bill. And Jimmy wants that new iPhone X.

But Brock can. No restrictions on him. Brock, who, unlike Jimmy, has a work-study job at Young Library that puts money in his pockets even though his scholarship is full-ride and he also has a paid job "interning" at Wrigley Media Group. Getting his foot in the door while he's still in school, collecting checks along the way. No prob.

"And if you think they're taking advantage of you?" Brock follows up. "Dude, the NCAA is *way* worse for the guys at those big schools that play football."

There's a right and wrong to Brock's belief. While the NCAA is reaping the most financial benefits from basketball, especially the NCAA Tournament—which, as of 2018, was bringing in over $800 million—the same can not be said for college's governing body for football. That money is shared among the conferences and schools directly, where, for example, in 2016, twenty-four of the top twenty-five money-making college football programs made more than $100 million. So, while technically the NCAA isn't way worse for college football players, it's the schools themselves that are way worse for the players. Which makes no difference to the players, because either way someone else *besides them* is making millions.

This bothers Brock more than most. Maybe more than it does Jimmy. Only because it affects Brock differently, though not directly. For that, he is on a mission. An eighteen-year-old Morpheus, "exposing fake shit."

See, Brock's last name is Williams. Yeah, the same as Gibson Williams, All-American safety at USC. In LA. Gib is Brock's older brother. Decided to stay home and play for the Trojans. He's LA through and through. Got Lakers and Raiders tats to prove it. A "Straight Outta LA" one, too.

Brock's watched his brother go through it at USC. Watched as USC has asked his brother to do *everything* for them. And not just on the football filed. Appearances, meet-and-greets, volunteer work on behalf of the university, public interviews, tour guide for potential incoming students, help recruiting. Yet, if Gibson went to someone in administration and asked for some sort of monetary compensation for all of the extra hours he's put in for the school and on behalf of the school, and someone found a way to cut Gibson, say, a thousand-dollar check, the entire football program would be under investigation and Gibson on USC's campus would be the new Reggie Bush. So Brock knows.

Brock's and Gib's father is from St. Louis, hence their names. He was a diehard baseball fan and player. Got as far up in the majors as AA, then shut his career down once his rotator cuff went bad. Started coaching baseball while in St. Louis. His name started floating around as a go-to guy on hitting. His nickname: Sensei. He came up watching and idolizing Rod Carew. California Angels, Rod Carew. So when he got a call from the Angels organization to be one of Mike Scioscia's hitting coaches in 2001, he straight up did the Beverly Hillbillies thing and headed West. Family in tow. The next year, the Angels won the World Series.

He wanted both of his sons to be the baseball player he wasn't. Didn't happen. Both Gibson and Brock loved baseball, but only because their father loved it so much. They were both on something different. Brock loved basketball, Gibs football. Both played their respective sports growing up and at Mater Dei High. Gibs became one of Mater Dei's "Hall of Fame" stars; Brock, as good as he was at hooping, got cut from the b-ball team his junior year. And it was because the Williams household wasn't using sports as a "gateway to their freedom"; Gibs and Brock weren't raised with an understanding or belief that sports was going to "save" them. They grew up having other interests, a much broader spectrum of reality than most other kids who are forced (or guided) into believing sports equals escapism. Their parents *taught them* choices.

Gibson chose to play ball, Brock chose to play the game. The "other" game. The game of a college student in America who wants to change what is accepted as "the norm" when it unfairly benefits those in power. Between the two of them they figured they could work out a way to not get taken advantage of by the NCAA. "Good luck with that," Jimmy told Brock once. Brock's reply: "I was brought up not to believe in luck." Which is the exact opposite of how Jimmy was raised.

The latest poster child is Hunter Greene. As *Sports Illustrated* labeled him, "A socially conscious high school short-stop starter who rakes, throws 102, and makes scouts believe in hardball unicorns." He is the latest phenom whose talents were headed to the NCAA. He, like Brock and Gibs, is from Cali, and like Gibs decided to stay and play, but for UCLA. He, like Jimmy, was on the cover of *SI* early. Before the true blow-up. Talked about as "next," often referred to as a "prodigy." A word Jimmy hates.

What separated Hunter from both Jimmy and Gibson is that he never attended UCLA even though he committed to, signed, and accepted the school's scholarship offer. He got a seven-figure ($7.23 million) advance signing bonus at seventeen years old. Because the entry rules in professional baseball are different from those of football and basketball, Hunter was able to enter into the MLB's minor league, after being drafted out of high school, and basically get paid for doing the exact same thing Gibson and Jimmy have been doing: playing at the purgatory level of their sport. In baseball's 2018 amateur draft the top four picks came straight outta high school. Their combined signings totaled over $27.6 million. An average of close to $6.9 million for each, while not playing on the game's biggest stage.

Part of the reason the NFL and the NBA haven't set up systems similar to what Major League Baseball has set up is largely because of the NCAA. Too much money is guaranteed by those two sports at the D1 college level for a baseball-like system to exist or be created. Any business model set up to circumvent the more than $1 billion the NCAA now averages in revenue would be like a Frank Lucas or Henry Hill messing with the Five Families' money. (In 2018 the NBA did decide to create a "Select Contract" to begin paying $125,000 to "elite" players in the G-League who want to skip college and play in the NBA's minor league equivalent for the one year they have to be removed from high school before entering the NBA Draft. But that $125,000 in comparison to what the "elite" players are signing for, going into baseball's minor league system, is basically a joke.)

Football and basketball broadcast rights amount to GNPs of small countries (College Football Playoffs sold the rights to broadcast the three-game, four-team series for $7 billion over twelve years), with shoe deals made by universities enough to feed small countries (Ohio State and Nike, $250 million for fifteen years; Kansas and adidas, $191 million for fifteen years; UCLA and Under Armour, $280 million for fifteen years; and so on). Payoffs, kickbacks, and scandals; coaches and scouts taking the fall for something much bigger; monies going everywhere to everyone except to the student-athletes responsible for upholding the archetype. It's not wrong so much as that over recent years what it really is has become a wrong more visible and egregious. So when Brock uses the "slavery" association, Jimmy gets it. Doesn't totally agree but fully understands the nature of the analogy and how it can be looked at by so many as such. After reading William C. Rhoden's *Forty-Million-Dollar Slaves* and Marcus Rediker's *The Slave Ship: A Human History* in high school, Jimmy knows where being taken advantage of ends and true slavery begins.

He tells Brock, "Your brother is at least lucky that EA ended *NCAA Football* before he got to USC. They were making mega-mils off that game and none of the players were getting *anything* from it even though their likeness was being used. They pro'ly woulda put Gibs on one of the covers, sold a couple-a-million copies and pocketed all of that."

"Yeah," Brock replies. "I remember in grammar school all he would talk about was what his rating was gonna be once he got to college. And how he was gonna destroy people by him playing him in the game."

The settlement of former UCLA basketball player Ed O'Bannon with the NCAA was the only reason the NCAA discontinued its relationship with EA Sports, which ended the life of the *NCAA Football* model. The 2014 lawsuit challenged the use of college athletes and their likenesses (not names) without compensation. The games generated millions annually for the company and the NCAA. Yet the players whose avatars were being used in the games were not seeing anything in financial return. Further, had an actual player asked someone affiliated with their school if they could borrow money to buy the game in which their likeness was being used so they could play the game themselves, the player's scholarship would be in breach and their actions considered an infraction of the NCAA's rules.

"And what's so crazy about that," Jimmy flowed, "is how the NCAA made money from the game by letting EA Sports use 'NCAA' in the title, and the players that made up the game and were used *in the game*..." His point faded into the darkness of the conversation. He just shook his head and went back to playing *Fortnite*.

His momma told him never put in work. His T-shirt same color as the Off-White Prestos on his feet. A gift. From unknown. He ain't saying. Tryna make money, making mistakes. Fucking up commas and karma. His college life, swerve-o; his NCAA life, owned. "Hard work leads to luck" is the oath he was raised on. His eyes all on the bag while all eyes on him. He listens to "1985" constantly. Watches *Love & Hip-Hop* religiously. Hoping that ain't his story. His "j" is cold. Dropping five 3's a game. The twenty-nine he averaged last year in high school was as easy as the twenty-six he's averaging now. The Baby LeBron comparisons have been replaced with the "next Jayson Tatum." He got Gus Johnson highlights to match his Marcus Smart high lites. They don't call him Chidi no more. He's "Manchild in the Un-Promised Land." He's living his best life.

Yet. At games the students at opposing schools would chant,

"Jump Jimmy Crowe! Jump!" reenacting the opening scene of the minstrel routine by Thomas "Daddy" Rice. Which the UK students in the crowd would do nothing to stop. Neither would the administration or officials at the opposing schools. "His momma gave him the name," one student at U of L said during their intraconference battle at Louisville. "She knew what she doing."

Jimmy heard it, but didn't hear it. At this point, to him, it was one of those things that kept his skin thick. Forced him to embrace not only the name he was given but also his Charlie Murphy exterior. Probably a little hypersensitive after talking recently to a McDonald's All-American teammate who plays for Duke, who put him up on a *Vanity Fair* story about young Republican white women on UNC campus who don't apologize for the president. The reason for the share of the story: for Jimmy to prepare himself for when he enters true hate territory. Beyond rival, beyond enemy. In this current America, there's nothing the school or coaching staff can do to prepare their players for what they may encounter. Jimmy's prayer during every game, when the chant would rear its truthful head: *Drop forty on these Trumps, and it will end.* Then he'd open his eyes. Never letting the tear fall that always formed. Back to the game. Darkness.

With an 11–3 record, and holding down a number-seven ranking in the country, there is talk around campus and in the media that Jimmy is definitely "one and done'n" once the NCAA tournament is over for the Wildcats. Mock NBA drafts have him going as high as number five. The hype is seeping into Jimmy's head. Still he's him.

A few weeks ago as part of his work with Wrigley Media, Brock got tickets to Camp Fog Gnaw Carnival in LA. Flight included. Hotel comped. Jimmy, who would have done almost *anything* to see Kanye and Cudi perform, wanted to roll with. Couldn't. He'd've had to come up with the money for the flight. Money his family two weeks out didn't have, money he couldn't "scramble up" without red flags being raised. Crossing that "anything" line seeped into his head. This is where the hype gets real. See, the organization (not university) that Jimmy plays for has those rules; rules that apply to students who take scholarship offers attached to athletics. Jimmy's suitemate, who is on a music scholarship, who is going to Fog Gnaw too, doesn't have the same school-based restrictions as Jimmy; Jimmy's chem lab partner—who probably thinks Fog Gnaw is a meteorological formation and has no clue who Tyler The Creator is—is on an academic scholarship and doesn't have the same school-based restrictions as Jimmy. See: theme.

And it is that theme that gnaws at Jimmy. It's his argument, problem with, disdain toward, and contempt for the whole "no-pay-for-play" debate. He understands that sports in academic institutions, especially with D1 CFB and Blue Blood programs bringing in millions through football and basketball, lends itself to and is wide open for corruption, but why the student-athlete has to "pay for" that possible corruption through the possible sins of adults is just wrong, in his eighteen-going-on-thirty-year-old mind.

"I don't want to be paid," Jimmy tells Brock in the middle of another one of their NCAA-deep conversations. "Getting paid is *not* the point! I low-key just want to have same freedom as you and all the other students on scholarship. That's all. The *shit* is simple."

Brock hears him and raises the bar. Only slightly because he is not walking in Jimmy's or his brother's shoes. And he knows this. He's not living their lives, not chasing their dreams, but he hears them say the same things. Feel the same way. Share the same whitewash.

"Here's the deal: the NCAA has you by the balls. We can be mad at them all we want, but the fact is they are just part of a system set up to basically own both the sport and the players that play those sports. We can't sit here and act like the NBA and NFL aren't a part of the system that allows the NCAA to keep functioning the way that they do. Look, Gibs and I have had crazy convos over the years, but I've never gone deep on basketball, and to me the way their system is set up, it's worse than football even though I still believe the colleges take more advantage of the players."

Brock's voice elevates. "Just the whole age limit, gotta be one year removed from high school, only drafted first round through the NCAA is cactus. Like, how the NBA gonna punish the player if the owners want to draft him? What kinda shit is that? With football at least they have their system in agreement that most if not all players aren't ready for the NFL until they've at least experienced playing at a certain level or in a similar system for two years. Like as good as Tua or Ed Oliver or Bosa are, owners know they ain't ready for the NFL. But the NBA? Dude, if they could take kids *before they get to high school*, they probably would. They thirsty as fuck. But . . ."—he takes a sip of Corona—". . . no, they don't take that out on the owners who can't control themselves. They set up a rule to punish the players, to not let them enter the league even though the demand is there for them to get in. And the NCAA supports that all day because it keeps players under their control longer and they make more money from that."

"Conspiracy much? So what's your alternative, 'Ock? Because ain't nobody really complaining. Like me. To me, it's just one year."

"My alternative is to put the onus on the owners instead of the player. If a team feels a certain player is good enough coming straight outta high school to ball in the league, then *that's on them*! Just have the teams pay extra to draft him. Like an extra luxury tax or some shit. Like, if the player is under nineteen, then you can draft him but it's gonna cost you an extra whatever million dollars. Charge these teams on the front end for *your* talent. You just said you can wait, but why should you *have to* when they are the ones desperate to get you? If an owner feels that *you* are worth it, if they feel you are right now ready to save or change their franchise and they don't want any other team getting dibs on you, then *they* need to pay for it."

"You on some reverse franchise tag shit," Jimmy says to Brock, laughing. "Gimme that Corona, fool, you starting to sound too much like Ice Cube's dad in *Boyz n the Hood.*"

Brock ain't laughing. He feels in his mind what he just said out loud can be more than theory, more than noise and rhetoric coming from some college kid. His mind tells him that his idea can be implemented. His heart tells him that it *needs* to be.

Suddenly Stokely, a junior from just outside Philly who at times kicks it with Jimmy and Brock, unleashes. Tired of them "personalizing" the whole NCAA thing, he big-pictures Jimmy and Brock's whole back-and-forth. Loudly.

"What about the Auburn softball team? Y'all know about that? Or what about how Michigan State basically covered up for the gymnastic doctor? Or how UNC had all of those athletes *for years* taking b.s. black studies classes to illegally make grade? Or how Urban Meyer—and I'ma say this nicely because I fucks with Urban Meyer—'downplayed' the whole domestic violence situation with one of his assistant coaches? Or, or, the thing at Baylor a few years ago, where the basketball coach basically had players lie to cover up one of the players' getting murdered? Not only that but the sex scandal of Baylor's football team? It was like fifty-two counts of rape. And I ain't even gon' mention that whole Penn State situation. Sandusky? Yet, that program still ballin'? You all talking this whole 'gettin' paid versus not gettin' paid' bullshit, when, real talk, the NCAA, as an organization, got problems. Major. *Much* more than *anything* you two keep arguin' about!"

Nothing else was said the rest of the night.

Dorm room party. Next day. Guzzling Old Tom gin. Listening to Billie Eilish. Mood.

Jimmy's turn. Stokely's words ran deep. He has his own Brock moment. Screaming at everybody in the room. *Grown-ish*. "Lemme just say this, the fact they can continue to get away with this is fucked up! And if none of you think this whole thing isn't about race, you all are stupid! Basketball and football are the two sports both at this level and at the next level that are predominately played by people of color, mainly by this, niggas!" He taps the side of his face.

Music pauses. "And our two sports are the only ones where the rules are basically enforced for us not to live a certain way? For us to live under the total thumb of a system while everyone else gets to have at least a controlled sense of freedom? What the fuck is that? And all we do is sit back and take it! And I know that new NCAA rule is gonna kick in in a few years, but that's bullshit too. There's still gonna be things we can't do that every other student on-campus can. We sign these letters to come here, knowing that what we are getting in return is not even c-l-o-s-e to what they are getting out of us. But that's cool. We all know we got to do this to get to the next level, even though only a small percentage of us make it to the next level. But that's a whole 'nother story."

Jimmy's teammate—nickname: Pillow, self-imposed because, as he says, people be sleepin' on him—is leaning on the wall about twelve feet from Jimmy, spittin' weak game to a young lady who reminds everyone on campus of TNT's Rosalyn Gold-Onwude. They call her Rose Gold.

"His ass. Always on some anti-Kumbaya extra," Pillow says to her. "Feel me?" He 'bout to get that bag from the league. Why he not just happy? I ain't getting drafted to the league, but I'm way more happier than his ass."

"Jimmy does have a point. The *whole thing* is messed up for you all. It's just he's one of the only ones to see it and say something about it. If *your ass* was smart, you'd listen."

Pillow looks down at Rose in a "Do you know who you are talking to?" sorta way. Trust. She does. Because before he even gets to respond, she shuts it down.

"And ain't nobody sleepin' on you *or with* you. So stop tryna play the victim and recognize who *you* are."

"From the way I see it, the unfairness isn't us not getting paid, it's that there are a different set of rules for us because we are athletes. Mark Zuckerberg was at Harvard and began raking in stacks for the Facebook concept before he dropped out, and no one said a thing because he didn't break any NCAA rules. The same with the dude who started the company of the cookies y'all are eating right now! *Insomnia!* Yeah, them shits! He and his boys started that while they were in their dorm room! No restrictions! And, uh, uh, what's her name, Brock? The singer that I like so much? Jazz? Used to play the bass? Went to school in Cali?"

"Esperanza?"

"Yeah, Esperanza Spalding! She was on music *scholarship* at Berkeley and made two albums while still a student there and signed with a label. But basketball and football players can't sign our own jerseys and get *anything* for it? All I'm saying is since none of these people who seem to be so smart at this can come up with a solution for paying us, at least let us live the same lives as all of the rest of the students that are getting a free education. I mean, I hear people keep saying that we are celebrities on campus while we are here, and most of the other students aren't. Well, most of the other students on scholarship aren't generating the kinds of money we are for the school while they are here. So that makes us even! Now can a nigga just get a work-study job so I can put something on this Tally-Ho bill?"

Laughter erupts. "Manchild snappin'" can be heard around the room. Mood? Changed.

"Keepin' it one *thousand*," Jimmy goes on, Old Tom bottle still in hand. "Someone really needs to do something about this. Like, straight up challenge the NCAA, the whole organization. And not just one player, I'm talking a real lawsuit, with thousands of us going against them. Some *Brown v. Board of Ed*–type shit. Seriously. I'm tired of reading all of these stories and hearing these dudes on ESPN and Fox Sports and sports radio talking about how 'we being done wrong' and how 'unfair the system is' to us athletes but *ain't no one doing a damn thing* to try and change it. I know y'all. Think I'm trippin' but this is facts. And as much as I love being here and being a part of this whole UK family, love Coach Cal, love my teammates, love Rose Gold if she let me, love everything I'm learning, love being away from home, away from Mississippi just so I can see how other people live, love not having to be an adult yet, I'm tired of—no disrespect to the women in the room—getting fucked. I'm tired of all of us getting fucked. Brock likes to call it slavery, but it's not. It's just one of the closest things we have in sports, in this country, to it."

With knowledge dropped, followed by the invisible mic, Jimmy looks at Brock, then Pillow, then Rose Gold. Finding approval. Rose walks over, puts her arm around him, Pillow curls up his fist and gives him a pound, Brock stays sitting on the bed, nods his head upward. "Everything I say should be a Travis Scott quotable, son!" Jimmy says, in his best Texas accent. He finally laughs. He's in his own *Astroworld*. And for the first time since he's been away from home, he realizes he's not alone.

In his dorm room a few days later, Brock, bored with studying, grabs one of the old magazines he'd stolen from his father's collection back home and flips across a story in *Sports Illustrated* about a guy he'd heard started this whole "sneaker business" thing with the NCAA. Sonny Vaccaro. He stops flipping. As a kid he kept hearing stories of how Sonny was like a mob boss. Original Soprano type. That when people actually saw him they'd kiss his ring. Same with that other guy, Worldwide Wes. ESPN had done a *30 for 30* documentary on Vaccaro that Brock hasn't seen yet, but he's heard about. And to him, if someone does a *30 for 30* on you, you are official. He dives into the story.

In the *SI* piece, Vaccaro says something to Dan Greene that makes total sense: "The financial arrangements between the universities and the shoe companies is the bottom line in this thing. How can they find seventeen-year-old kids guilty of some goddamn thing is beyond me. The coercion starts at the top. If the school wouldn't have wanted the player, if the shoe companies wouldn't have wanted the player, if they all didn't want the player. . . . My prayer would be to get enforcement out of the NCAA's hands and come to their senses and allow these kids to earn money while they are playing sports," he says. "I think that's going to happen. Because it'll happen again. Some kid's gonna take something tomorrow. That's what human nature is."

From there Brock falls deep down the rabbit hole. Sicko mode. He researches the details of the O'Bannon 2014 antitrust lawsuit levied against the NCAA. From there he researches Kain Colter's 2014 "unionization" case and the National Labor Relation Board's 2015 rejection of the case. Which leads him to learning about Ramogi Huma and Tim Waters and the NCPA, the National College Players Association. From there he learns of Jeffery Kessler's 2017 $208 million antitrust win against the NCAA. He studies, for three straight days, the 1890 Sherman Antitrust Act.

Then, as Brock discovers, the b.s. really hits when University of Oklahoma QB Kyler Murray wins the Heisman Trophy.

Murray, even after being drafted by the Oakland A's with the number-seven pick in the 2018 MLB draft (same draft as Hunter Greene) and signing a $4.7 million contract, was able to maintain his amateur status in football for the remainder of his scholarship at Oklahoma and play for the school because of a "rule" in the NCAA rulebook. A rule that states: "A professional athlete in one sport may represent a member institution in another sport and may receive financial assistance in the second sport." Yet let one of Murray's OU teammates try to make money off the field doing something "non–sports related," and the proverbial shit would hit the Lennox. This is the situation that drives Brock forward.

A week later Brock walks into the 100 Funkhouser Building and changes his major to law. His epiphany. His vision: to represent both Jimmy and Gibson as clients in a case against the NCAA. Something the NCAA can't stop even as they're attempting to, as the chair of the NCAA Board of Governors put it, "embrace to provide the best possible experience for college athletes" and change the criteria to pay-*while*-play. This is something the NCAA can't stop—even as, a year from this moment, the association will attempt to change the criteria for representatives hired by players entering the NBA. It may be ten years from now, but Brock knows. It hits him that there is a reason he is in this position to hear and be connected to both sides of the NCAA story. Best friend and brother: victims turned plaintiffs. Not that Brock wants to be a lawyer or anything, he just wants to be at the center of change. Someone who unwrongs the wrongs. He's always felt this whole thing was another form of slavery, and this last week of reading and researching has only verified it. A young man finds his calling.

Scapegoats. Sinners. Victims. Violators. Big bank swallows small bank. Spits out. Exposed. But not really. Iceberg. Tip of. Stripes. Swooshes. Under Armour. Under the gun. Under the right and left arm of laws being broken. Men in black: suits versus skin. Can't stop. Won't stop. Too deep in. Ingrained. Fabric. Blood. DNA = NCAA.

Truth told. Brock has figured it out. Ball is life, except when someone or something owns you.

CHAPTER 10

#BASEBALLSOWHITE

Making a Curious, Theoretical, Disturbing, Outrageous Case for Jackie Bradley Jr.

In the 2018 MLB postseason, there was a coming-of-age story that went totally unacknowledged. Not only for what it was but for the possibility of what it meant. Boston Red Sox outfielder Jackie Bradley Jr. had a coming-out party. One that should have made him the focal point of a long overdue movement in baseball.

A black dude emerging in America's eyes as potentially one of the game's next superstars. Not a brotha from somewhere else, not an import, not a baseball phenom scouts went over to find in Cuba or the DR or somewhere deep in South America. Naw, this was a black AMERICAN ball player. Born and raised. The kind that over the years has become nearly extinct at the major league level. Sure, his teammate, Mookie Betts—another black American baseball anomaly, who was just weeks away from being crowned the regular season MVP of the American

League—had reached superstar status, but JBJ was the one who, at the moment, was taking baseball out of its unidimensional look. He'd just won MVP in the 2018 ALCS, with his stock, visibility, and notoriety on the rise. Making him more the future than the present. He was set to finish what Brandon Phillips started—being baseball's newest black superhero. Condensed to a singular meaning, Jackie Bradley Jr. got next.

Or does he? Over the course of what is now going into its second generation, there have been many Jackie Bradley Juniors who were positioned to change the current baseball narrative. The Upton brothers, Curtis Granderson, Matt Kemp, Lorenzo Cain. Even with everyone from MLB Players Association executive director Tony Clark to White Sox former GM and current executive VP Kenny Williams to Diamondbacks outfielder Adam Jones (who publicly called baseball "a white man's sport" in 2016) championing the "cause" to get more ball players "like them" in the majors, until the last two seasons the percentage of black American players in the MLB has hovered near record-low levels—a huge contrast from the early '80s, when almost 19 percent of the league was black. The first question that should be asked: Why is there even a "got next?" As in: Why are we in search for a black savior in order for black Americans to make a pilgrimage back to baseball? The second—and more important—question that should be asked: Why hasn't there been a movement? A *real* one. One with the word "matter" attached to it, to indicate that the lack of black American ball players in baseball *does* matter. For everything that baseball has historically meant and represented to black people in America—and to America itself—you would think that there would be more—some!— real noise about the generational decline of African American players' participation and interest. But there seems to be little. Very, very little.

In 2016 African American players represented 74 percent of the NBA, 68 percent of the NFL, and only 6.7 percent of the MLB. This, coming from a league that less than a generation before had a larger percentage of African American representation in the game than it did in the country, in a sport that to this day is singled out as a catalyst at the forefront of the civil rights movement. Jackie Robinson, Larry Doby, Hank Thompson, Willard Brown. And while the NFL and NBA have over the last few generations ascended to greater levels of popularity and stature, baseball is still called "America's game" for a reason. More than any other sport, it represents the best and worst of America; the era when America was at its racial, political, economic, and ethical worst—and when sports had the true power to change that.

Not that Jackie Bradley Jr. (or, say, Tim Anderson) can save black baseball or change the way MLB operates, but he (they) can represent the essence of saving black baseball. In him lies the hope of black baseball's future. Because if he's not the one with the power and potential to resurrect our fate, who is? Jordon Adell? Xavier Edwards? Look, here's the best way to put into radical, overblown, and probably flawed perspective how "bad" things are and how desperate a call for attention, action, and activism should be: currently, of the MLB Top 100 players list that *Sports Illustrated* did in February 2019, prior to the opening of the spring training season, only seven were African American (same percentage as that of players in the league), and of those seven only two were in the Top 50, with Betts at No. 2. Jackie Bradley Jr., the one who holds our future on his bat and in his glove, came in at No. 96.

Over the course of the twenty-plus years that I've been covering sports, I've been asked constantly, whenever the subject comes up, "Scoop, are there solutions to this blacks-not-in-baseball thing?" My answer, never what anyone wants to hear: "Nope." Sometimes I'll respond, "Not really," even though I don't see a solution in sight. It's too far gone, too deep rooted, and no one is upset or concerned enough to make the needed pivot from the direction the game is going without us.

And I say that because what I *honestly feel* doesn't address the causes for or a possible change in the way that baseball has always minimized our role and importance. From the reductionist role the game played by never acknowledging the importance of Larry Doby's sharing Jackie Robinson's color barrier–breaking space to the lack of interest paid to the public push to make Satchel Paige's Kansas City home a historical landmark, baseball has made it historically clear how it views the relationship of blacks and the sport. I'm always like, "Where's the 'George Bush doesn't care about black people' Kanye when he's needed?" A cry for reality. Then I remember, there's no crying in baseball.

Lawrence Hogan pretty much confirmed my pessimism in his National Baseball Hall of Fame and Museum book, *Shade of Glory: The Negro Leagues and the Story of African-American Baseball.* He wrote:

> By early 1933, the future of African–Americans in baseball was increasingly doubtful. Conditions and salaries for players were at their nadir, and the professional league structure [for blacks] begun by Rube Foster over a decade earlier lay in tatters. Simultaneously, white organized baseball continued to maintain its unwritten exclusion of black athletes. As in other areas of African-American life during the Depression, the question arose whether blacks should now focus their attention on protesting against white discrimination or continuing to build their own institutions.

Slogan: Baseball and blacks—it is what it is, gonna be what it's always been.

There will be those—such as Richard Justice, who penned an article for MLB.com in 2013—who protect baseball from analysis like this. Justice opened his column with the following absoluteness:

> Baseball's commitment to civil rights is on display every single day of every single season in the dugouts and executive offices across the sport. In the end, it's that simple. There are men and women of color and different backgrounds and experiences leading the game, shaping it, instilling it with their vision. Once the ceremonies have ended and the speeches have been forgotten, that is what civil rights is all about. After a weekend of emotion and remembrance in which Major League Baseball honored the courage and vision of the people who were on the front lines of the fight for racial fairness in this country, it still comes down to actions, not words. Baseball's progress in this area is indisputable. It has long been intertwined in America's civil rights struggle. Jackie Robinson broke the sport's color line in 1947—one year before President Truman integrated the Army, seven years before the Supreme Court's *Brown v. Board of Education* decision, and nearly a decade before Dr. Martin Luther King Jr. began leading the fight for fairness. As King once said, baseball forced Americans to see the world in a different way than they'd seen it before. There would be miles to go when Robinson played that first game, but it began with an African-American man playing a baseball game.

So true. But in this current state, so meaningless... to those who pull the strings. This made it interesting when, in the same column, Justice quoted one of the string pullers, one of the very few owners in the game with a black person in a "seat-at-the-table" position within a MLB organization. "It makes you feel that baseball has been more than just a game, more than just a recreation," White Sox owner Jerry Reinsdorf said. "We had a great impact on the country." Love the fact that he said "we." Gotta love inclusion.

There will be those in baseball who disagree with this theory of minimization or feel that African Americans should simply be grateful to the game and what it's afforded us. As if Garrett Morris's Chico Escuela ("Baseball been berry berry good to me") was a real ex-player and not a character he played on *Saturday Night Live*. Dave Zirin, in his book *Welcome to the Terrordome*, subtitled a chapter about the US government and former NFL player and Army vet Pat Tillman "How People in Power Exploit the Games." Truth is, the people who play the game have been exploited, too, ever since the game's inception. It's agenda setting at the highest level, perfected. Baseball is no different from politics, owners and executives no different from politicians. As Zirin wrote, "It's easy to forget how people in power use sports to advance their narrow agendas." Even easier to forget when the agendas are widespread and hidden in plain sight.

And since numbers seem to be the thing now in drawing conclusions based on theories, here are two I like to look at when considering white people's sustaining of power and control in baseball. The first is pitching. The position of pitcher in baseball (very much like the QB position in football) is the game's most treasured, protected, and coveted position. For black players, the number of pitchers has never risen above 7 percent. Recently (2016), according to the Society for American Baseball Research's latest data, it is somewhere between 2 percent and 3 percent. And while position players and everyday players remain the highest paid and most honored in the game, the game still revolves around pitchers, and they are still (and always will be, just like the QB) the most valued and respected. This is a barrier that to this day black ball players have found it almost impossible to overcome. The second is the draft. I'll use the 2017 and 2018 MLB drafts as samples of their commitment because, as we all know when it comes to sports, nothing proves how serious a league, team, or organization is about their future than how they build their franchise. In 2017, of the thirty players selected in the first round of the MLB draft, there were four black players drafted (Hunter Greene, No. 2; Jordon Adell, No. 10; Jeren Kendall, No. 23; Bubba Thompson, No. 26). In 2018, that number decreased to two (Kyler Murray, No. 9; Jordyn Adams, No. 16). So, how serious can the major leagues be about increasing the percentages of black Americans when the top black talent in North America is not considered a priority investment? Prior to the 2017 draft, between 2012 and 2017, according to *USA Today*, 20 percent of the players drafted in the first round of MLB drafts were African American. That number is going down. And no one seems concerned.

Some I know will ask, "Well, why aren't whites complaining or making a big deal about the decline in number of white players in the NBA and NFL?" Answer: Because ownership has not changed. Because the power structure in those sports has not changed. Because the reality of who really runs shit has not changed. Because outside of what happens on the field or on the court, everything else for the most part in those sports remains the same. Control of those leagues still belongs to whites; there's no reason to complain or have concern. And while the same can be said about the control of major league baseball, the fact is that, unlike the NBA and NFL, the decline in the number of black players is an issue for black Americans because that's the only foundation of power we have in the sport. And historically in America, through sports, we—African Americans—grow. Or at the least, find some leverage. In the MLB, at this time, that "some" presents itself in the form of only two black team presidents (Kenny Williams, Chicago White Sox, and Mike Hill, Florida Marlins) and one black GM (Dave Stewart, Arizona Diamondbacks). And because that leverage has been so reduced, Shohei Ohtani will soon be the new Frank Thomas . . . *and* the new CC Sabathia . . . *and* the next Miguel Cabrera . . . *and* the next "King Felix." The *new next* Negro. The new nonwhite player who will have a Hall of Fame career but no direct impact on advancing the culture of the game for the advancement of his people. Which is why the lack of a movement behind the dropping percentage of blacks in the game is disturbing. Not that black players need to "take over" the game the way America feels we have basketball and football, but the black presence in the majors—on and off the field—should be more reflective of our historic worth and contribution. In baseball, whites still make up 64 percent of the players in the game, at least 70 percent of the players in the game's most powerful position, 99.99 percent of the highest-ranking chief executive positions in the league, and 100 percent of team ownership.

It all adds up to the continued minimization mentioned earlier. A hindrance that acts as functionality.

History is the proof.

Yet, the game remains one of my favorite sports. Making me the hypocrite Kung Fu Kenny spit about at the end of "The Blacker The Berry." Habitual. Stereotypical. Finding myself concluding, on some days: "Hey, at least baseball isn't as white as sports radio."

Which at most times leads me to the conflicting conclusion that I may be wrong. There may be hope. There may be a solution. Even when there are no screams, no outside action, no movement or pushback from the people, no hashtag. Hence, maybe—*maybe*—when a black player (aka Jackie Bradley Jr.) gets one of those Mike Trout/Bryce Harper/Manny Machado/Gerrit Cole bags (contracts), we will fall back into baseball's nucleus. Money is the root of all evil, but it also is the root of our chase. Once there are greater odds of getting one of those

$200 million or $300 million contracts, black American talent may turn its attention back to baseball. Until then the numbers of us in MLB will probably remain the same. Because I know how black folks are, when it comes to numbers, especially in sports: we always play the percentages.

> "Yet when you look back, what people didn't realize, and still don't, was that we got the ball rolling on integration in our whole society."
>
> —Buck O'Neil

If ever a truth was spoken, that would be it. People forget that it was Dr. King who *thanked* them—former Negro League players—for giving him the blueprint and strength to fight the fight. Baseball and boxing (beginning with Jack Johnson, then Joe Louis) were the early progenitors that normalized black people in the eyes and minds of white America. Baseball was where blacks literally, to a large degree, leveled the playing field. It was America's game, and it was one of the first places where we leveraged the two-fifths of us that was yet to be considered human. Which is why the decline of black participation in baseball to such a low level is meaningful. Blacks in America always speak about the power of our vote and how we had to fight to get the right to vote—well, the fight we put up to play baseball was not that far removed. Our soul was in the game, our soul shaped the game. So it's on us to recognize the symbolic nature of our current situation, and although we may not agree on the *practice* we must take into consideration the necessity associated to the circumstance.

As when, in the midst of MLB's acknowledgment that the drop in number of black players was a problem, they announced that they'd retained the search firm Korn Ferry to assist in the interview preparations of qualified candidates for "key baseball

operations positions" with "special emphasis [on] the prepara-
tion of minority and female candidates." Seriously. As if the
Selig Rule (named after then commissioner Bud Selig), put in
place in 1999, wasn't enough. Apparently *not*.

Baseball isn't so white because of the numbers, baseball is so
white because of the way the numbers are controlled. Especially
at the top. At the MLB plateau it comes off as almost a plot, or
a more fitting word, a ploy, to keep the numbers of nonblack
Americans at a certain level. A controlling number. The "ploy"
behind this could be power, rather than race or nationality. White
power. As if to have black Americans hovering around 20 percent
in the game was a threat. One that made them look at what eventually happened in the NFL and the NBA and say, "Oh, hell naw!"
They don't want to lose control of the game the way the NFL and
NBA have; they don't want the players leveraging and exercising
their power in their league the way they have grown to do in the
other two leagues. And part of the power nonwhite players have
amassed in the NFL and NBA comes from the majority percentage that non-white and African American players hold in both
leagues. So MLB got strategic, smart, and slick and found ways
to stabilize or reduce African American involvement and interest.
Institutional. Structural. Control.

Enter the new. From South America, the Dominican
Republic, Puerto Rico, Cuba. When MLB's African American population was at its apex, the Latinx and Latin-associ-
ated population in the game averaged in the 10 to 11 percent
range, from 1967 to 1983, according again to the SABR. By
2009, that number had ballooned to 28.5 percent. A percentage that remained similar as the 2019 season began. For the
"new Negroes" that baseball has chosen to replace the original
ones, there's a "happy to be here" attitude it seems MLB is not
only taking advantage of but also enforcing. Again, the Chico
Escuela theory. It's more ideology than fact, but the optics...

damn. It *looks like* and often *comes off as* "MLB goes out of its way to seek talent everywhere outside of America, and places in America where blacks *aren't*, before they seek in places and spaces where black American talent can easily be found."

In a 2007 CNNMoney.com piece, "Green Behind the Decline of Blacks in Baseball," then MLB executive vice president Jimmie Lee Solomon openly admitted, "Clubs do leverage their dollars much better if they develop a kid in a country not subject to the draft. Those decisions are purely business decisions, very pragmatic business decisions."

The problem is how that only seems to affect the American ball player of non-white, non-European, non-rural-living, non-US-privileged, non-melanin-challenged, non-seat-at-the-Trump-White-House-table descent. In going back to the trend that seems to be occurring in the MLB drafts, the 80 to 90 percent draft rate of white American boys into the game is not impacted in any way by the same "very pragmatic business decisions" Solomon spoke of. Baseball is a $9 billion industry. There's financial room for advanced domestic diversity. So either balance the economic and cultural playing field for blacks and whites in America when it comes to baseball, or treat the game here in the urban communities the same way it is treated by MLB in Latin communities outside of the US. That is if they are honest about wanting change, which they continue to make it hard to believe they are.

The other problem is, the numbers back this asinine theory up, as does the fact that all thirty major league teams have *at least* one baseball academy in the Dominican Republic while a significantly smaller number exist in urban areas across the US. The drastic decrease on one side combined with the constant increase on the other can easily lend itself to a preconceived case of color-coded, nationalistic paranoia. Making a curious, theatrical, disturbing, outrageous case for the next black American player up to bat to save our existence in the game. Which isn't the smartest thing to say or write in a book. But sometimes smart has to take a backseat to risk; sometimes complex evidence takes a back seat to what something we see makes us *feel*. And baseball in the major leagues makes many people feel a certain way. So much that even legendary baseball Hall of Famer Joe Morgan once had to admit: "For a black kid, I came to the conclusion that you're better off living in Cuba to get to the big leagues than you were living in the United States."

Even so, what we can't do is pretend that MLB is acting alone in this conspiracy. Not on this one. We—African Americans—are more co-conspirators than victims. We abandoned baseball. Period. Even with possibly good reason, there's still *that* truth we must both face and admit. We no longer saw baseball as a primary "escape route" to the athletic, sports–dominated black lives that mattered to us. Once the NFL seriously started drafting kids out of HBCUs (Michael Strahan, Jerry Rice) and the NBA started making the drafting of kids straight outta high school (Kobe Bryant, Kevin Garnett) a thing, the baseball route to freedom was over for us. Black parents and black kids in America found every reason and excuse possible to steer away from baseball as a life choice: "It's too expensive," "It's too time consuming," "There's too much travel, it's not stationary enough," "The schedule is too hectic," "My kid doesn't have his father around to teach him how to play," "There are no black men in the black community for him to play catch with," "There's no baseball field in our neighborhood for him to learn how to play," "I tried but he lost interest," "Not enough of the players on the team look like him," "None of the players on my team look like me," "The coach is racist and the league he plays in is too," "The other players don't want to be friends with me," "It's easier to get a college scholarship in basketball and football than it is in baseball," "He can make more money in football and basketball," "It's too much work for him to be successful," "Ain't no black superstars in baseball," "Baseball is boring." And we still exist in that space. Even with MLB and individual teams in MLB implementing Reviving Baseball in Inner Cities (RBI) programs and Amateur City Elite (ACE) programs and the Youth Academy, along with the Diverse Business Partners and Diversity Fellowship programs, we still disguise excuses as reasons. Thems just the facts.

Of course, facts can be both gift and curse, used for good or evil. The fact is that baseball in the majors looks and feels as if it no longer needs or wants us, and we no longer want or need it. This is the game's harshest reality. It's not necessarily *true* but it is *real* and has been shaping into a reality for a while now. The MLB may have perfected it, but black folks allowed it. It's the pill we don't want to swallow, the mirror we don't want to look into, the actuality we don't want to own. One that even Jackie Bradley Jr. might not be able to fix. So, just say that if this current baseball circumstance—as compared to the Academy Awards and the #OscarsSoWhite movement that *forced* another segregated, monocultural, discriminating, insulated, self-governed, white-male-legislated industry to acknowledge our participation, contributions, and history (catch the analogy?)—were a movie, it wouldn't be *Bingo Long* or *Soul of the Game* or *42*, it'd be Jordan Peele's *Us*. Because when we sink into the abyss of all this, we—African Americans—are our own worst baseball enemy.

CHAPTER 11

FAKE NEWS

The Tricknology of the Great American Sports Argument

We argue. That's our thing. That's how we who happen to love sports get down. We live in an "embrace debate" culture that forces us to take sides on almost all things when it comes to sports and also allows the media to play a larger-than-life role in dictating what these arguments are and the direction those arguments should take. Yes, it's controlled to a degree, and, yes, the basis of many sports arguments (much like political arguments) is so topical that diving beneath the surface doesn't seem necessary. But in a majority of cases, it is. Yet we fail to dive, often going no further than what the news cycle of the moment tells us.

This behavior is called "media system dependency." Introduced as a theory by Sandra J. Ball-Rokeach and Melvin L. DeFleur in 1976 in a paper titled "A Dependency Model of Mass-Media Effects," media system dependency theory offers a framework for how audiences depend on media information to meet needs and attain goals. A group's dependence on information from outside media (print, television, radio, advertising; now including the internet, digital and social media, and more) increases as that medium supplies information that is more central to the group. The paper also goes further into how the cognitive, behavioral, and affective (mood) results of the audience are often functions of the degree to which they are dependent on media-driven information.

Basically, the media, both mass and social, tell us something and we buy into it. Often without challenge. And because of that we, the audience, far too often fail to take *all things*, all information, into consideration when drawing conclusions or forming opinions involving certain sports stories. Especially ones that lead to great, polarizing sports debates: LeBron. Terrell Owens. Derrick Rose. The Patriots, the good and the bad. Antonio Brown. Age limits. The one-and-done rule. The b.s. of the BCS. Pay-to-play. Instant replay restrictions. #baseballsowhite. A lot of it is misunderstanding, a lot of it is on us for not diving deeper to be better informed about what we believe. Comparative analysis can often redirect a narrative. Or, at least, can make us look at those narratives in a different way. In sports, because of the culture of debate that constitutes so much of the public's involvement, juxtaposing one debate against another has become a lost art.

It's basically taking what's presented to us as fact and as truth without challenging the presentation. Not settling for what we are being led to believe. Sometimes, it is good to make a case for the other side, for the opposite narrative. Sometimes, it is simply good to take all things into consideration before embracing the debate.

To support this are four examples of sports storylines that, over a period of time, have taken on lives of their own. Stories that at least on the surface seem to be ones where comparative analysis, open-mindedness, and a measure of inclusion of all of the information could make the argument a NMFF. (Shout-out to Evelyn Lozada of *Basketball Wives* for the abbreviation.)

1. TIGER WOODS VERSUS ROGER FEDERER:

For the most part, even though both are considered the greatest ever in their respective sports, it is general consensus that Tiger Woods is the greater overall athlete/sports figure of the two—Tiger being in the GOAT conversation, Roger being in the GOAT *tennis* conversation. Most would even argue that Tiger was over the course of his career more dominant. In the argument of overall greatness, it's weird how it's almost automatically *assumed* that Tiger Woods's greatness easily eclipses Roger Federer's. The question that has been and will continue to not be asked: Based on what?

A template:

Woods, 1997–2008: fourteen major championships, six second-place finishes, three third-place finishes, twenty-four finishes in the top ten.

Federer, 2003–2014: seventeen major championships, eight second-place finishes, eleven semifinals (third/fourth) finishes, five quarterfinal (top eight) finishes.

(And Roger still holds in his sport the most grand slams for a male tennis player, with twenty, two *ahead* of the second-place player, Rafael Nadal; Tiger is second in his sport for male golfers, with fifteen, three *behind* the leader, Jack Nicklaus.)

Woods (as of 2018):
    Went ten years without a major, 2008 and counting.
    2014:   0 wins, 0 second, 0 third, 1 top twenty-five.
            Ranking, number 25
    [Note: began the year ranked number 1]
    2015:   0 wins, 0 second, 1 third, 3 top twenty-five.
            Ranking, number 257
    2016:   0 wins, 0 second, 0 third, 0 top twenty-five.
            Ranking, number 652
    2017:   0 wins, 0 second, 0 third, 0 top twenty-five.
            Ranking, number 1,199

2018:   0 wins, 1 second, 0 third, 3 top twenty-five.
          Ranking, number 13

Federer (as of 2018):
      Went four-and-a-half years without a major, 2012–2017.
      2014:   0 wins. 1 second, 2 semifinals, 1 fourth round.
                Ranking, number 2
      2015:   0 wins, 2 second, 0 semifinals, 1 quarterfinal, 1
                third round. Ranking, number 3
      2016:   0 wins, 0 second, 2 semifinals, 2 missed. Rank-
                ing, number 16
[Note: Out of the top ten in ranking for the first time in
fourteen years]
      2017:   2 wins, 0 second, 0 semifinal, 1 quarterfinal. 1
                missed. Ranking, number 2
      2018:   1 win, 0 second, 0 semifinals, 1 quarterfinal, 2
                missed. Ranking, number 2

Overall:

Tiger in Majors, 1996–2018*
      14 titles
      6 second-place finishes
      24 top-three finishes
      31 top-five finishes
      (25 twenty or below finishes, including 8 missed cuts)

*finished final two in three of four majors at least five times.

Roger in Slams, 1998–2018*
      20 titles
      30 finals
      43 semifinals
      53 quarterfinals

*reached finals of each major at least five times.

Now, of course, there have been injuries that Tiger has
dealt with over the last five years that have to be taken into
consideration. That's fair. But let's go back prior to Tiger's

injuries and the "incident" that had as much to do with derailing his career as his back surgeries. This isn't subjective, these are just facts.

A sample: at their heights, during similar eleven-year periods, beginning with the year both won their first majors. Both hold records for total and consecutive weeks as the number-one players in the world in their respective sports, but the one thing that sides with Tiger is his *total* number of weeks on tour during his career that he's held the top spot. It more than doubles Roger's.

> Tiger: 683 total weeks at number 1
> Roger: 310 total weeks at number 1
>
> (Tiger: 281 consecutive, Roger: 237 consecutive)

But again, Fed's fall has not been close to being as epic or damaging.

There was a stretch during his career when Federer went eight years in Grand Slam tournaments, 2005 to 2012, never losing before the quarterfinals. For Tiger there was an eight-year stretch, between 1997 and 2004, when fourteen times he finished *outside* the top ten in majors, seven of those outside of the top twenty.

Then there's this: from the beginning of his career in 1998 through the end of the 2018 season, Federer only missed four major tournaments. Woods, even before the injuries that have basically eroded the last five seasons of his career (pre-2014), missed six majors and missed the cut in two. And before anyone goes apesh*t with "Well, what about their overall tournament/tour records?," as of the end of the 2018 golf season, Tiger over the course of his career has amassed eighty victories. Roger, over the course of his? Ninety-eight.

(Tiger's total PGA career wins: 107; Roger's total ATP career wins: 150.)

Part of dominance and greatness that gets lost in many arguments is consistency. And over the course of their careers, Federer has been far more consistent at both finishing strong and being on the court than Woods has. The numbers in this case don't lie. They're there for the public record. Damn shame no one has taken the time to look further into it.

But this is America at its most typical. Creating a narrative where someone from America is at the beginning and the top of any and all conversations concerning greatness and dominance. This is one of those rarities where Americanism trumps race, color, ethnicity, and gender. We've seen it in the global treatment of Wayne Gretzky (Canadian!) versus other GOAT American athletes. We've seen it with Usain Bolt versus Michael Phelps. We've seen when America took the name football from futbol. And how this country continues to make sure the American version of the sport remains far more relevant than what the rest of the globe embraces as the world's most popular sport. This is simply how this country rolls. Especially when it comes to sports and sports figures, and how those teams, players, and events will be historically remembered.

2. KEVIN DURANT VERSUS THE WORLD

Chasing a false legacy instead of "earning" one. That in the larger sense is what Kevin Durant was targeted as doing, before his move to the Brooklyn Nets in 2019. His decision to join forces with the Golden State Warriors in the summer of 2016—a season after almost defeating them in a playoff series that his then OKC Thunder team was leading 3–1, and on the heels of the Warriors' NBA record-setting seventy-three-win season and seven-game Finals loss to a Cleveland Cavaliers squad led by Kyrie Irving and LeBron James—dropped a bomb on the sports industry that caused a reaction many say hadn't been felt in generations, if ever. Durant caught hate. That's the simplest and only way to put it. His manhood was publicly challenged, his heart put out to pasture. His decision was basically called "the weakest move any athlete has ever made." Followed mostly by the universal sentiment that "the greats do not run from challenges, they face them." Until they die.

This comment by BlueTeepee in July 2016, in response to a Mika Honkasalo story on HoopsHype.com entitled "How the Warriors Got Kevin Durant and What It Means For the NBA," sums up the general feeling about Durant's move:

> If he stayed at OKC, he would have had all the chances to make it happen, especially after [the] Ibaka excellent trade. And in case he would have made it, he would be [counted] as a hero and filled with love and appreciation by the local fans. Now everyone outside Oakland hates him, he is considered as a coward by going to a team that beat you instead of showing the character and try to do your best to beat them back. Something that would never happen had he stayed at OKC or even moved into a smaller club with big ambitions to have a new challenge. For now, the championship ring, which he'll most likely win, will mean almost nothing.

Underneath the hate lives a belief that had Durant decided to re-sign with OKC or go to another team that wasn't as great as the Warriors, that team would have stood a strong chance of dethroning the Warriors in the Western Conference or dethroning the Cavs and doing the same thing to the Warriors in the NBA Finals that LeBron and Company had just done. Which is so far from the truth, if we are keeping things 1000. The belief that KD had a chance at winning an NBA title had he not joined the Warriors is about as improbable as winning $1.6 billion in the lottery. And there are facts to validate this that both the general public and media choose to ignore, forget, or never take into consideration.

Fact 1: Golden State was not going to be the same team the next year regardless of whether or not KD signed there.

The Warriors had money. The way they'd structured themselves going into the 2016–2017 season under the cap, plus with the cap expanding from $70 million to $94.1 million, *plus* with no player on their roster taking up 20 percent or more of the cap (now, max players can take up to as much as 35 percent of a team's cap space), Joe Lacob, Bob Myers, and company had money to go out and add a max-level player to their roster. That they were definitely going to do whether or not they'd won the chip that year. With that, know that had Durant not signed with the Warriors, going into the 2016–2017 season there was a *very, very, very* strong possibility that Al Horford, DeMar DeRozan, Bradley Beal, Eric Gordon, Andre Drummond, or even Dwight Howard or Hassan Whiteside (who were both highly coveted at the time) would have been added to the Warriors' roster. None of them demanded the money in the open market that KD demanded, which means had the Warriors signed one of them, the team would have had money left over the next season to possibly go after *another* right-under-the-max major free agent. Basically, a team that OKC, even with Durant and Westbrook, would not have stood a chance at defeating.

Fact 2: Russell Westbrook never guaranteed that he was going to remain in OKC with KD if KD decided to stay.

Just as there was, according to Durant, never a moment when he told Westbrook (or anyone on the Thunder squad) that he was "coming back to the Thunder," Westbrook, whose contract was up the following year, in 2017, never confirmed with Durant that he was going to re-sign with the Thunder. This often represents the missing puzzle piece when the whole Durant-leaving-OKC conversation hits full throttle. Predictable scenario: Durant signs either a five-season max deal to stay with OKC or he and his agent structure a one-plus-one max-player-with-option deal similar to the one he signed with Golden State, and the following season he and Westbrook *don't* win an NBA championship or they don't beat the "new look" Warrior team that KD decided not to join, and the following off-season Westbrook decides to cut out, to play elsewhere. Where does that leave Durant? Exactly! Either in OKC without Westbrook, in a five-year deal with no chance of joining that dynasty unless he does what DeMarcus Cousins does two years later and signs with the Warriors for a year at veteran's minimum (one year, $5.3 million)—which, looking back on it, would have ended up being a total loss for Durant of around $56 million—or not being on the Warriors at all, as they couldn't afford him the next season because they went out and got someone else once he declined their offer. Either way, Durant stood a greater chance of being ass-out of a ring if he'd stayed with OKC.

Fact 3: KD would have been looked at as the biggest fool in the history of free-agent sports had he turned down the Warriors offer and never beaten them, regardless of what other team he decided to sign with.

During the process, Durant had meetings with five teams outside of his meeting with the Thunder, and he said that he was going to be "selfish a bit" in making his decision—both clear indications that he was at the very least "open" to seeing what other teams had to offer and what basketball life would be like for him outside of Oklahoma City. The pitch made to KD by the Warriors was legendary. While the phone call from Draymond Green immediately after their Game 7 loss to the Cavs, followed by the "Hamptons visit" from Green, Steph Curry, Klay Thompson, and Andre Iguodala, got all the headlines, there were personal conversations with Jerry West and his previous history/friendship with Warriors assistant coach Ron Adams (who was one of Durant's coaches at OKC from 2008 to 2010), and all of these played a part in Durant's decision. And, just saying, had news gotten out after the fact that those four players showed up at KD's door in the Hamptons to recruit him *and* that one of the greatest, most respected GMs in basketball history—the man who *is* the NBA logo—called to recruit him, *and* that he had a chance to be coached *again* by one of the greatest assistant coaches and defensive minds in NBA history, and he turned all of that down, the hate and contempt directed at Durant would have been replaced (by the same masses of people) by labels of stupidity and incompetence. People—media included—would have simply rephrased the "weakest" move in NBA history as the "dumbest" move in NBA history.

Also, KD wasn't the first or only elite player to be in the middle of something like this. There have been two other situations in NBA history that come very close, but neither player (nor situation) caught the same amount of public heat or scrutiny. One because it was done by trade, the other because there was a two-year separation from the playoff defeat of the team the player left and the one he decided to join forces with.

The first was the 1982 trade of Moses Malone from Houston to the Philadelphia 76ers. Unlike KD when he joined the Warriors, Malone was the reigning NBA MVP when the trade took place, and, also unlike KD, the team he was coming from had lost in the NBA Finals the year before. But just like KD, Moses was summoned to a team that had lost in the NBA Finals the previous year and was on a mission to win a ring. The Sixers had just lost to the Lakers in six games in 1982 (remember, the Warriors pre-KD had just lost to the Cavs in seven games). They felt that they were one player away from beating the Lakers. Now, did they need to go out and get *one of the best players in the game* to make that happen? Did they need to add the league's reigning MVP? No. But they did. And on the flip side, in order for Moses to finally win a ring, did he have to join a team that already had two future Hall of Famers and leave a team was only two years and three games removed from possibly winning its own NBA title? That's questionable. Bottom line, had he wanted to, Moses could have vetoed the trade or he could have asked to be traded somewhere else. But he didn't. He knew the career and personal legacy value that came with his going to the Sixers and forming a superteam. One that had the capacity not only to (easily) beat the super-team that had come together in LA but also to be considered one of the greatest in the history of the game. Which, eventually, it was.

[Author's note: Now, we could include Wilt Chamberlain leaving the Sixers and joining forces with Jerry West and Elgin Baylor on the Lakers in 1968, with sights on teaming up to beat Bill Russell and the Celtics, but it would be petty to go that far back, right?]

The second was Chris Paul's 2017 free-agent decision to leave the LA Clippers and join the Houston Rockets. A squad that (*very much* like the Warriors/OKC in the 2016 playoffs) defeated Paul's Clippers team in 2015, after being down 1–3 to them in the series. True, Paul's decision was two seasons removed (the Clippers had failed to get out of the first round the subsequent two years), and the Rockets had not won the title, but the idea that Durant went "running to the team that beat him" is also exactly what Paul did. Only CP's decision wasn't as immediate, and was separated by two other playoff falloffs. But he still ended up joining—by choice—the same basic team (one that included James Harden) that his former team had a 3–1 lead on, only to bow out and down to. Leaving behind, like Durant with Westbrook, an All-Star player (Blake

Griffin) to fend for himself in the quest to win a title.

Did Moses Malone have his situation held against him? No. Has Chris Paul had his decision held against him? No. But in the minds of most: *Durant is the devil.* Is it the two years' separation from when CP lost to the Rockets that made it OK for him to have done what he did in order to get a ring? Is it the fact that Moses was traded and not a free agent that differentiates his joining a superteam in order to get a ring? Technicalities. It's just weirdly interesting how the KD hateration is singular, while others have avoided the same venom.

3. JIMMY BUTLER VERSUS THE MINNESOTA TIMBERWOLVES

NBATV host Jared Greenberg perfectly labeled this episode "Jimmy Eats World": Jimmy Butler decides to play the victim in an attempt to force the Minnesota Timberwolves to trade him on the premise that the young core players the organization was building around "don't want to win" or "don't know how to win."

The media, as divided as the stunt came off during this episode, painted Butler as a gladiator, old school–type of superstar with the killer, winning mentality that is missing from this current generation of superstars. This storyline, promoted by the media, became one of the main narratives that opened the 2018 NBA season only because no one seriously challenged Butler publicly about his claims and reasoning.

(Eventually Butler was traded to the Sixers, thirteen games into the 2018 season, but the chaos leading up to the trade is where the fake truth of the story resides.)

Let's go through a timeline:

April 25, 2018: Timberwolves' season officially ends. They lose to Houston Rockets in five games after making the playoffs for the first time in fourteen years.

July 13, 2018: "They said, 'You guys have done everything and we're very appreciative, but our bet is that we should wait 'til next year and we could get ourselves a better deal.' ... We did everything we could, and they want to do what they think is right for Jimmy."—as told to Glen Taylor, owner, after Butler declined an extension.

September 17, 2018: Butler meets with head coach and team president Tom Thibodeau in LA. Demands trade.

October 10, 2018: Butler shows up to practice for the first time since the trade demand and drags the third-string squad to victories against the starters. Humiliates Karl-Anthony Towns. Then yells at Wolves GM Scott Layden, "You fucking need me!"

Beneath the surface it's all fake, all something it really isn't. Butler's "lifting his leg" act (as phrased by NBA analyst and former player Tim Legler) worked enough to create a "well, he does have a point" theory about the weak-soft-heartedness of Andrew Wiggins and Karl-Anthony Towns, but the misdirected narrative Butler created allowed him to do the following: 1) to escape being looked at as the leader he wasn't trying to be, and 2) to sidestep the fact that the non-max extension the Wolves put on the table to him in July (four years, $110 million as opposed to the rumored four years, $145 million he was seeking or the five years, $188 million he could have re-signed for going into the 2019–2020 season) was the real reason he decided to act a fool. For a player like Butler, who has built a rep for being "all about the game," not to fully commit to a team or to the game because of money would do more damage to his rep than anything he did to embarrass or emasculate his teammates, Thibs, or the Wolves organization.

Since Butler tried to focus the drama on what his teammates "weren't about" and what they "couldn't do," accusing the players around him of not wanting to win, let's look at how that claim doesn't hold weight, at least not as the sole reason that Butler, as reported, was demanding to be traded. This is where the media failed to go "in" on Butler with proof—*on-the-court proof*—that those "specific" players weren't as *dedicated to winning* as much as he.

- Against the Rockets during that playoff series, Butler only led the Wolves in scoring once, in Game 3: twenty-eight points.

- In two games during the series the leading scorers for the Wolves were Wiggins, with eighteen points, and Nemanja Bjelica, with sixteen points.

- James Harden, Butler's primary defensive responsibility in the series, scored as follows: forty-four points (Game 1), twenty-nine points (Game 3), thirty-six points (Game 4).

- Karl-Anthony Towns led Minnesota two games in scoring and in all games led them in rebounding.

Yet Butler was given a pass to vent. And in the media's coverage, Wiggins was one of the targets of Butler's revolt; Wiggins was one of the players who wasn't "holding his own"; his heart pumped Bai. In that series against the Rockets, here are Butler's per-game numbers compared to Wiggins's:

Butler: 15.8 points, 6.0 rebounds, 4.0 assists
Wiggins: 15.8 points, 5.2 rebounds, 2.0 assists

There's a specific focus on that series because it was the last time (prior to the beginning of the next season, when the Wolves failed initially to meet Butler's trade demand) Butler played with the team. Keep in mind, he came to this team as a missing puzzle piece that was supposed to get them to the playoffs for the first time in almost a decade and a half. Which he did. That's growth, part 1.

The Wolves came into those playoffs as an eighth seed, playing against not only the number-one seed in the conference but the team with the best record that season in the NBA. The chances of the Timberwolves beating the Rockets in that series were Zig-Zag thin. The fact that they won a game off of the Rockets was a minor miracle in itself. Growth, part 2.

Growth, part 3, was supposed to be the 2018–19 season, the final one of the two-year deal Butler had left on the trade that brought him back to play for Thibs, to finish what they had started in Chicago before Thibs was fired by the Bulls in 2015 and took over all things basketball for the Timberwolves in 2016. The "deal" was for Jimmy Buckets to lead the young Wolves, show them the way to get it done, and take them *through the steps* of what it takes to win in the NBA. Steps that he and Thibs both knew would take time, at least two years. Butler was supposed to be the Yoda of their "process." But Jimmy checked out midway. And true Jedis don't check out.

Typically, in order to start calling out other players—especially teammates—for not performing at a certain level, the stats of the player making the complaint should be far greater than those of anyone he or she is calling out. In the case of Jimmy Butler, a three-time third-team All-NBA player who had finally received a single MVP vote in 2018 and came in tenth place for the award that year, the numbers tell a story of a man who was honestly in no position to call out anyone, without including himself, based on performances in a playoff series that only he as the leader of the team had been through before. So for him to make an example of his teammates for what they aren't capable of doing, when he wasn't on some Jordan/LeBron/KD *'ish* from a playing standpoint, was kinda, well, "not cool, bro."

And the bigger problem? The lack of fact-based research by mainstream media—with all of this analytic, deep-dive data at their disposal—to find where the fault fell in Butler's claim. No one saw fit to redirect Butler's narrative and call out his cop-out for what it was. Worse? No one inside the Timberwolves organization called him on it, either. In sports, true leaders and those who follow their lead know that patience is not just a virtue when it comes to building a team, it is a necessity. They also largely own up to their part of the deal. In Jimmy Butler's case, "the deal" was for him to play for Thibs for two years and see where he was able to "lead" the young Wolves, then either sign a re-up to stay there or bounce to be closer to getting a ring and/or movie deal. But Jimmy aborted that. He straight up did everything he could to dodge his responsibility, putting the onus on ownership and management to relieve him of his "Jedi" duties while orchestrating an "I see the bitch in yoo" scenario against others without name-checking himself in the song.

But we, because of the aforementioned and other reasons, didn't challenge Butler, either. We fell for the whole "Jimmy Butler has that warrior mentality that these young, spoiled, pampered-ass players don't have" bait. We, again, found selective fault and applied *said* selective fault when fault wasn't close to discriminatory. Jimmy Butler made a power move and it worked. Not that he ended up getting everything out of it what he "wanted" but he did do something that made "we" believe that the problem was them, not him. Which had to be enough of a win… for him.

4. JAY-Z AND THE NFL

"Truthfully I want to rhyme like Common Sense
(But I did five mill)
I ain't been rhyming like Common since"

—"Moment of Clarity"

"Being broke is childish and I'm quite grown"

—"I Love the Dough"

"I bought every V12 engine
Wish I could take back to the beginnin'
I coulda bought a place in Dumbo before it was
Dumbo
For like 2 million
That same building today is worth 25 million
Guess how I'm feelin'? Dumbo"

— "The Story of OJ"

"In the race to a billion ($), with my face to the ceiling
with my knees on the floor
please Lord forgive him
Has he lost his religion?
Is the greed going to get him?
He is having heaven on earth, will his wings still
fit him?
I got the Forbes on my living room floor and I'm
still talking to the poor
Nigga, I want more"

—"Grammy Family (freestyle)"

"On the holiday playin' 'Strange Fruit'
If I'ma make it to a Billi ($), I can't take the same
route."

—"Oceans"

"Takes a nation of millions to hold us back

But when your boy reach a billion ($) it's a wrap."
—"A-Billie" ("A-Millie" remix)

"Slayin' day in and day out
When money play in, then they play you out
Tryin' to escape my own mind
lurkin' the enemy
Representin' infinity
With presidencies…"

—"Dead Presidents"

"While y'all playa hate we in the upper millions
What's the dealing (huh)
It's like New York's been soft, ever since Snoop
came through and crushed the building
I'm tryin' to restore the feelings
fuck the law, keep dealing
More money, more cash, more chillin'
I know they gone criticize the hook on this song
Like I give a fuck
I'm just a crook on this song"

—"Money, Cash, Hoes"

"I'm a hustler, baby, I'll sell water to a whale"
—"U Don't Know"

"I can't help the poor if I'm one of them"

—**"Moment of Clarity"**

Funny thing happened when Jay-Z crossed the imaginary line of cultural consciousness and decided to cuddle up and get all cozy with the NFL: the black "anti-NFL" base that rides with Kaepernick the way Trump's base rides with Trump lost their #IMWITHKAP minds. Even those who were anti-Kaep caught feelings.

"Sellout," "backstabber," "conspirator," "treasonist," "self-ish," "self-serving," "hypocrite" were the terms used when the story broke, invoked across spoken and written platforms, both social and broadcast media. Eric Reid said the move was an "injustice" to the movement he and Kapernick started; lawyer Mark Geragos, who represents Kaepernick, called the deal "cold-blooded," saying Hov crossed the "intellectual picket line." The *NY Post* claimed it was the "perfect cover for the NFL's 'social justice' movement"; *The Undefeated* wrote, "No matter where Jay (Z) started, he's now got more in common with NFL owners than with NFL players"; Chance the Rapper, on *The Breakfast Club* radio show, said that if asked by Jay-Z to perform at a Super Bowl halftime show, that despite his love for Hov, "Naw, I wouldn't... I don't think the Super Bowl is my actionable item"; author and activist Shaun King openly said he was "deeply disappointed." Even though people from Cardi B., Diddy, and Killer Mike to Stephen A. Smith, DL Hughley, and Michael Eric Dyson understood and publicly supported the Jay-Z/NFL partnership, the overall consensus was that Hov had turned Burr. #Traitor.

But what was missed the most, by most, was the inaccuracy of that belief. Hov never turned; Jay-Z never dissociated himself from who he was, who he's always been. In the overtelling, undertelling, and misstelling of the same story, somehow the conclusion was drawn that Jay-Z was now different from the person he had shown himself to be over the course of this life of his: Shawn Carter made that NFL deal, Jay-Z didn't. Jay-Z founded Roc Nation, Shawn Carter runs it. Yet we fell for a fictional tale built on expectation—of a black superstar, a God MC—who throughout his career has told us constantly in his lyrics (see: bars) who he is and what he's really about. And even though the media play on this was to find fault with Jay-Z, the truth is, the fault lies within us. Seeing what we wanted him to be instead of what he has always been.

Jay-Z, over his career, has masterfully presented himself as an icon of cultural change, but it's what Shawn Carter positioned himself as that was at the center of the partnership with the NFL. And although the NFL should have been further exposed for race-shaming (think of Steve Harvey's, Kanye West's, Ray Lewis's and Jim Brown's photo-op meetings with Trump) the public belief that Jay-Z was a singularly socially woke/aware artist who represented black and brown injustice was a narrative as misleading as the idea that Kaepernick's protest was about the flag. When it comes to social and racial restitution, Jay-Z is woke; when it comes to money and power, S. Carter is wide awake! Just trace the path: Roc-a-Fella Records was followed by Rocawear clothing (which he sold for $204 million in 2007, yet he remains the CEO); followed by the opening of his 40/40 Club (a sports bar); followed by the partnership with Live Nation Entertainment that launched ROC Nation; followed by a four-year deal with Sony Music; followed by his purchase of Armand de Brignac (Champagne brand, valued in 2019 at $310 million); followed by the global partnership deal with Universal Music Group; followed by his acquisition of Aspiro (tech media, for which he paid $56 million), which he turned into TIDAL ($600 million value in 2017); followed by *Forbes* announcing his reaching the billion-dollar threshold in 2019. The hip-hop culture's first "mogul" to do so. But we were out here thinking he was going be a community within our community, that a mogul and his money would see things *differently*. In his own words: "That's where you'rewrong."

On one hand, there's the underlying belief that the real story of the partnership lies in the intersection of expectations, insight, and objectivity. That this is not Spencer Strasmore on *Ballers* trying to be the first black person to have ownership of an NFL team, this is a real brotha with real access to *real* money working his way to infiltrate the most exclusive (and arguably racist) club in American sports. As I wrote in a related piece for ESPN on the subject: "For Jay-Z, his seat at the table with Roger Goodell is not about cultural appropriation and racial reparations as much as it is a first step toward that exclusive power of ownership. As in: Jay-Z putting himself in position to be the first black team owner in the NFL. You can't put it past Hov. You all had to know that's what this was all about. *This is what moguls do.*"

On the other, his ROC Nation is the same company that had a partnership with the Weinstein Company (TWC) to tell "our" stories through film and has a former TWC executive, Patrick Reardon, serving as the company's current executive vice president of television. It's the same company that hired Demi Lovato's and Nick Jonas's manager, Patrick McIntyre, as the company's president of management. Heavy hitters. Heavy hitting. Major business moves by a company on the come-up to be a major player in the game. With all of this in mind, with the diversifying of a business portfolio functioning at this pace and level, why should we be surprised by their saying "yes" when the NFL came calling?

Two years prior to the deal, in the *Atlantic*, Spenser Kornharber gave us cultural warning in his review of *4:44*

Finding virtue in what appears to be selling out has, of course, long been part of Jay-Z's package. His list of corporate partnerships over the years is lengthy, and Sprint is the *third* separate phone company through which he's released an album. Many music listeners are, understandably, squicked out when an artist so enthusiastically links their work to corporate interests. But *4:44*, Jay-Z's best album in a long time, tries to answer those concerns. It's the thoughtful refinement of a career-long argument that Jay-Z has made: that for him, making huge bucks serves a greater good.

Dr. King, in his *Letter from Birmingham Jail,* wrote something that all blacks, regardless of class, status, income, fame, or ambition, must accept as our reality: "'Wait' has almost always meant 'never.'" How long, in the mind of Jay-Z, must we wait? I'm sorry, must "he" wait? He, Shawn Carter. One of only four living black billionaires in America. Because, lest we forget, it was also MLK who said, in his 1967 speech, "Casualties of the War in Vietnam": "There is an element of urgency in our re-directing American power. We are now faced with the fact that tomorrow is today. We are faced with the fierce urgency of *now.*" And nothing says *now* to a black self-made billionaire than an opportunity to be a part of a *real* billionaire boys club. Jay-Z invested in Pharrell's; S. Carter invested in R. Goodell's.

Nothing else in this book speaks to the power moves that can be made through sports to attain power more than this. It's just too bad the souls of black folks was the cost. As D.L. Hughley said about the NFL in the ROC Nation aftermath: "To them it's, 'If I can't own a black man, I can rent one.'" Our problem is that we felt they were "renting" Jay-Z, forgetting that Shawn Carter is the one making the moves.

"*Motherfucker, I—will—not—lose,*" (on "U Don't Know"). That's a Shawn Carter lyric.

At the end of the day, this whole thing should have been a non-story. Fake news at its cultural best. If we all just took the time to not make Jay-Z into someone he isn't and stop expecting the NFL to function as something it *really* isn't, then we'd realize all this was was a strategic move by two businesses trying to take advantage of one another at the other's expense. One billionaire trying to offset the other. Capitalists will do anything for clout. Because the chorus of Jay-Z's focus decodes all we all needed to know: it ain't ever been about where he's been, but where he's about to go.

Sometimes we're just suckas. Fools to the game. We fall for the cognitive dissonance of the spin power the media has to dictate the direction of our conversations. We know better but don't put in the work in to *do* better. There's no fun in that. No one wants to kill the argument. As explained by Ball-Rokeach and DeFleur's dependence theory: "The media themselves often create ambiguity. When ambiguity is present, dependence on media increases." Rationalization, overrated.

It boils down to what you can make an argument for and how fair and comprehensive you want that argument to be. The single thing they (the media) don't want in the culture of debate is for you (us) to "build a case" against an argument or line of thinking that challenges the merit of the argument or narrative to the point that you (we) rethink the purpose of it or draw the conclusion that this really should not have been a debate at all.

That would not only kill the message but the proverbial messenger as well.

CHAPTER 12

THE "NUMB" IN NUMBERS
How Analytics Is Becoming the NBA's New Jim Crow

Paranoia is a disease.

By definition it breeds in suspicion and mistrust. Makes you at times question activity, behavior, and motives without evidence or justification. Some of us *live* in paranoia. We honor the neighborhood.

In an interview with Charles Barkley during the 2015 NBA All-Star Game, the paranoia between us had reached a certain level. The interview never ran, for several reasons— some political, some personal. But mostly there was this philosophical difference between numbers and culture. An "us versus them" thing. And usually, in the "us versus them" world of sports and sports media, "us" generally takes the "L." At that time, the marriage of analytics and basketball had hit the fan. It'd been years in the making, but Barkley's going after Houston Rockets GM Daryl Morey—and my cosigning Barkley's stance—drew a line in the concrete that basically made purists and pundits take sides. And shots. At each other.

[Sidenote: ESPN.com editors at the time claimed they

didn't want me out there looking like an uninformed novice. With analytics basically being their new "brand within the brand," having one of their own challenge the methodology of a movement they were at the forefront of building would not have come off as smart business. Regardless of the basis and structure of the counterargument. Regardless that there's room for the counterargument. Regardless that there is another side to the story. And secondary usage rights would not allow us to reprint the Barkley interview for this book.]

This is where the paranoia comes in. The paranoia that rightfully exists in the integration of applied analytics to a game that probably more than any sport is ?uestloved in creativity, open-mindedness, performance innovation, and culture. Black American culture, to be specific. *As if* we hadn't seen this play before. There's a feeling surrounding the "forced" influx of analytics in basketball that revises history. A history of replacement, a history of takeover, a history of cultural appropriation and white society doing what it has historically done to black "contributions"—artistic or athletic, technical or theoretical, indigenous or ingenious—that they can't totally control. So the interview that Barkley and I had was simply one of many "Uh-oh, we see this coming again" conversations. We peep the covert, the master('s) plan. Which makes us just two basketball slaves not going down without a fight.

And while Charles and I exist in a historical state of paranoia that what rock and roll was allowed to do to the blues, what Elvis Presley was allowed to do to James Brown, or what cultural appropriation has done to hip-hop provide conjectural evidence of what could happen to basketball in this new analytical mind-set, the other side of the pendulum swing is a paranoia that the truth of what we've discussed in a larger dynamic will make enough sense to stunt not only the analytical momentum but the movement as a whole. A movement that over the course of the last decade has been a gateway of inclusion for white men in basketball that hasn't been seen once Earl Lloyd, Chuck Cooper, Sweetwater Clifton, Harold Hunter, Don Barksdale, and Hank DeZonie were "allowed" to play in the NBA.

Endgame: We play the game (even at the NBA level) for a greater purpose than numbers. There's a passionate connection we have to basketball that no other race, creed, or culture in America could understand unless it has walked with us through that four-hundred-year fire we call our existence in America.

And, still, there will be those who ask why race is involved or being brought up as a (or *the*) nucleus? The dynamics of the two sides forces it. The percentage of blacks playing in the NBA versus the percentage of whites who hold positions in the NBA rooted in evaluating talent and building teams through analytics. This raises questions about the balance of power: Who *really* has it? The player who plays the game or the person who dictates how the game is going to be played?

Each is a threat to the other, and the other *knows* it. Paranoia goes both ways.

Paranoia is also a hypocrite. During the MIT Sloan Sports Analytics Conference in February 2018 (SSAC18), on the "Take That for Data: Basketball Analysis" panel, the great writer/podcaster Zach Lowe said, "You can quantify some parts of effort."

Now, as much as that may be true at this stage of basketball analytics, the question is this: is it really necessary or meaningful to create such a metric when simply looking at a player's effort, movement, and desire with the naked eye, via film study or in-game situations, is enough to tell you all you need to know about a player's effort efficiency? *Either a muthafucka wants it or he/she doesn't.* Applying numbers and equations to determine how fast he/she gets through picks or cuts without the ball on pick-and-rolls or how fast he/she gets to 50/50 balls seems like intellectualizing the game just for the sake of intellectualizing it. Does the game really need a separate version of quantitative analysis to figure out what effort should look like? Or what effort is?

During another panel, "New Rules to Transform the Game," at the same conference, Mike Zarran, assistant GM and team counsel of the Boston Celtics, said this: "It's also the case for a long period of time the League did not have a culture of innovation."

Well, to millions of us the *culture* of basketball more than any other sports is *innovation*. But it's not the innovation that occurs through the integration of statistical modeling, computation, and player tracking. It's innovation by way of creativity, the purpose of play. Yes, the world loves Michael Jordan because of the standard he set for winning, but it loves him just as much for *the way* he went about it. Ways that will never have the same impact if you judged his basketball history by some metric on a spreadsheet or by "what the data says." As Virgil Abloh of OFF-WHITE fame and current artistic director of Louis Vuitton menswear said, "Michael Jordan is my superman. A larger-than-life character doing things that seem impossible. He proved that hard work, dedication, and being fearless works 100 percent of the time if you apply it to a dream or goal you have. What he did in basketball inspires me creatively."

At the center of what Abloh is saying are "fearlessness" and "creativity," words that don't align themselves nicely with the often over-thinking of efficiency that is at the roots of analytics.

And while what Mike Zarran says about innovation may be true, it presents a problem for those of us who look at the game for everything it brings to us, not just the numbers it has the ability to generate.

So far I've dropped a few names in order to make a point. You never want to call anyone out for their opinion (especially if you know them and/or respect their work), but one thing I've learned in this game is this: you are eventually going to make someone collateral damage at some point in time, or you are going to be collateral damage in a point someone else is making.

Feel my point. This was written by Neil Paine for FiveThirtyEight.com in February 2016, with the title "Russell Westbrook Wasn't Supposed to Get Better Than Kevin Durant":

> That leaves only three other MVPs in NBA history (not including Durant) who were overtaken by an existing teammate as their team's best player . . . *Kobe Bryant, who was (ducking as I type this . . .) outplayed by Pau Gasol on the 2008– 09 and 2009–10 Lakers. . . .*

Full stop, right? No need to go into whatever came after that statement, correct? Yet in his piece Paine had supporting evidence that Gasol "statistically" *outplayed* Kobe over the course of those two seasons. (Overall, Gasol's PER was better than Kobe's during the 2009–10 season and his win shares and win shares per forty-eight minutes were higher than Kobe's in both seasons.) And while we'd all be hard pressed to find anyone— including then Laker coach Phil Jackson, Kobe, *or even Gasol himself*—to cosign Paine's use of data in service of this belief, in his mind and on FiveThirtyEight's website, there was proof.

That "proof" lies directly at the root of the problem that analytics has brought in its takeover of sports, in particular in the game of basketball. As a society we have reached the point where we believe just about all the peripheral and superficial bullshit we are being fed. Right now, it's numbers. Mathematics, analytics, metrics, data big and small. The DREAM mentality. And while data rules everything around me, *we* decided that resistance is by any means.

Too many empty theories, too many number crunchers, too many pseudo-intellectuals, too many white dudes stripping away at the culture of the game by using numbers to dictate how the game is going to be played, and to discredit the way it was played in the past. It is the customary American process of controlling someone else's American Dream. Prioritizing efficiency over creativity by monitoring the workforce to divert even more profits for owners and shareholders by "quantifying the labor" in a way that squeezes every last drop out of the people actually doing the work. Leaving no allowance for individuality: *everything* must be accounted for. Consultants look at spreadsheets and decide who gets laid off, regardless of the people involved; the mandate is to get rid of (trade) a worker (player) at any time if their "numbers" aren't right, regardless of their importance to the company (team). It's nonstop surveillance. Your every move (whether as a basketball player, assembly-line worker, office worker, or doctor) is being tracked and then analyzed by somebody. Or, what's scarier, by an algorithm, with life-altering career decisions made by the few someones who know how to decode that algorithm. They've even found a way to turn "potential assist" (yes, you read correctly, "potential assist")—meaning a direct pass to someone who actually *misses* a shot—into a meaningful stat.

Leave it up to the analysts and they'll keep forcing this on us until we all believe it as fact. You can see it in the saying, "You can't teach speed or height"; or this one, "Numbers don't lie." The real truth is: You can teach someone *how to use* their speed and height, and while numbers don't lie, they hardly ever tell the whole story by themselves. Or the story that *needs* to be told.

The key to analytics (even according to Michael Lewis, author of the sports analytics bible *Moneyball*) is to "value" players and "evaluate" strategies by "using data to find knowledge."

No room for feel. No room for soul. No room for the spirit or the emotion or the intensity that speaks to why Kawhi Leonard and Giannis Antetonkoumpo are the players they have become, regardless of their PER, VOR, win shares, and usage percentages.

No room for the commitment to the game that often separates legendary from great and great from good. No room for intangibles or improvisation. No room for risks. No room for anything but the reduction of basketball players to a detailed series of numbers. No room for freedom.

> Basketball is working like the brain, where now—you're describing this research—as the ball moves around the court, we're going to know the expected points value of that possession, moment to moment. Which suddenly means you gotta pass that ball to the open man right there. Now we're actually saying the expected points for that possession go from .69 to 1.1—and that's how you win a game. Which is what we all want to know.

> So the fact of the matter is the best knowledge we have is that complex now—or a lot of it is. It's not categorical, it's not emphatic, but it's insightful as heck.
>
> **—Henry Abbott**

But how complex is it to keep it 1000 with the info being dished out and sold?

Example 1:

[John] Hollinger [the inventor of PER] joined the [Memphis] Grizzlies last December. A month later, the team raised eyebrows by trading away [Rudy] Gay, its leading scorer and most popular player. The criticism was loud in many NBA circles, but Memphis remained steady, entered the playoffs as a fifth-seed and upset the top-seeded Oklahoma City Thunder to reach the conference finals. Hollinger declined to specifically address Gay but said in general, "I think there's a better understanding of what is a high-value player or a high-value shot versus just what looks good."

That was from a 2013 *Washington Post* report about the NBA's embrace of advanced analytics and how the Moneyball movement was taking over the league. And here is the bogusness: they never mentioned or took into consideration that Russell Westbrook DID NOT PLAY in that series for OKC due to the season-ending injury he suffered in the prior series against Houston. Nor did they talk about how not having a proven twenty-points-per-game scorer or go-to scorer against the Spurs—their offensive go-to in that series to replace Gay was Quincy Poindexter—in the next round was one of the main reasons Memphis was swept. (Also of note: since the trade of Gay, a player whom "analyticals" basically have marked as, according to the *New York Post*, "the NBA stats movements poster child for an overrated player... the symbol of the overrated, overpaid player in today's NBA... one of the prime examples in the argument that high-volume, inefficient shooters are counter-productive to a team's ability to win," the Grizzlies have only been to the Western Conference Semi Finals once.)

Example 2:

The Houston Rockets—led by general manager and analytics buff Daryl Morey—are renowned for their use of data. The team rarely shoots long-range two-point jump shots, as they believe it to be one of the worst strategies in basketball. And their reasoning makes sense: the shots are too far away from the rim to be rendered a high-probability scoring opportunity, yet not far enough—as in behind the three-point line—for the risk to be rewarded with an extra point. This ideology, backed up by mountains of data, is a prime example of analytics at work. The Rockets were successful despite an injury-plagued season, losing in the Western Conference finals to the Warriors.

That was from the *Atlantic*'s 2015 "Welcome to Smarter Basketball" piece. It made solid and "smart" points about the new wave of analytics in the game but conveniently hid the truth that being "injury-plagued" had nothing to do with the Rockets getting dragged in the WCF versus the Warriors. It never acknowledged the other essential reasons why that series was over in five games, or why, even with Chris Paul, despite the 2018 playoff injury that took him out of the final two games of the Rockets series versus the defending champs, the Rockets haven't found a way to out-Warrior the Warriors. That said, here is the bogusness: the Rockets were out-rebounded by thirty-eight rebounds, out-assisted by thirty-five, out-scored by forty-one, out-shot by .460 to .437 overall, out-threed 37 percent to 33 percent, and had a per-game differential in points of more than 8. Add to that, also not mentioned, the reality that James Harden, not injured in the playoffs, scored only seventeen points in Game 3 and fourteen points with thirteen turnovers in Game 5 of that series.

Examples 3 and 4: Post-Game 3 NBA Finals 2016, via the ESPN Stats and Information Department
Kyrie Irving had a great Game 3. He scored efficiently, set up his teammates, and was even effective on the defensive end. His performance was so far away from how he usually plays against the Warriors (and in general) it would be surprising if he can continue to play at that level.

Scoring Efficiency:
-   In Game 3, Irving had an effective field goal percentage (efg) of 54 percent while scoring 30 points on 25 shots.
-   He shot 7.5 percentage points better than an average shooter, given the shots that he took.

- In all other games against the Warriors this season, Kyrie did not have an efg above 40 percent and shot at least 8 percent below what an average shooter would have, given the shots he took.

Distributing:

- In Game 3 Kyrie set up a shooter on 14 percent of the Cavs possessions he was on the floor for, and his teammates had an efg of 95 percent on those shots.
- In four other games against the Warriors this season, Kyrie set up shooters on 12 percent of possessions he was on the floor for, and his teammates had an efg of 34 percent on those shots.

Defense:

- In Game 3 Kyrie matched up against Steph Curry 34 times, and the Warriors scored only 94 points per 100 possessions and limited Steph to 21 shots per 100 possessions.
- During the rest of the season, Kyrie matched up against Steph on 89 possessions and the Warriors scored 119 points per 100 possessions and Steph had 27 shots per 100 possessions.

So perhaps Kyrie will continue to play better than he ever has against the Warriors, but the numbers suggest that he is likely to come back down to earth.

Only to follow it up two games later with this Post-Game 5 NBA Finals 2016, same source:

Kyrie Irving had an amazing Game 5 performance, scoring forty-one points on only twenty-four shots. The numbers tell us, though, that his performance was more of an aberration than a level of performance that he will be able to sustain into Game 6.

- Kyrie had an effective field goal percentage of 80.4 percent in Game 5.
- Over the past three seasons, Kyrie has had sixty-

three games in which he took at least twenty shots.

- In those games, Kyrie has never had an efg above 80 percent and had only four other games above 70 percent.
- If he had performed as he normally does, he would have scored only twenty-five points.
- Based on the quality of the shots he took (including defender distance, shot type, and shot location) an average player would have had an efg of 45.5 percent on the shots he took in Game 5.
- Over the past 3 seasons, Kyrie has taken 480 shots with a shot quality in the range of the shots he took last night, and his efg on those shots has been 46.8 percent.

Kyrie had 13 drives (15 drives per 100 possessions) in Game 5 and scored 1.6 points/drive.

- This season, Kyrie has averaged 1 point per drive—the same as his average over the last three seasons.
- Over the last three seasons, Kyrie has had 98 games in which he has had at least 13 drives per 100 possessions; he did better than 1.6 points per drive in four of those games.
- If Kyrie had performed as he usually does on those drives, he would have scored nearly eight fewer points.

Kyrie clearly overperformed last night, and while it is possible that is a prelude of performances to come, the data suggests that instead, he will return to being the good—but not great—scorer that he has been the last three seasons.

Here's the reality: Kyrie did not "overperform." Kyrie did Kyrie. He did what true "ball players" do, something data doesn't seem to take into consideration. The bogusness here lies in everything Kyrie did to counter what their "numbers" were saying he wouldn't or couldn't do again, and in just how wrong the numbers were in evaluating the type of player Kyrie truly was. And is.

Advanced bogusness:

Kyrie's Game 6: twenty-three points, four rebounds, three assists, two steals, two blocks, with a +25 +/-

Kyrie's Game 7: twenty-six points, six rebounds, one assist, one steal, one block, with a +10 +/-

And, oh yeah, that series-ending, championship-winning, historic three-pointer with fifty-three seconds left that won the Cavs the title, the one that the *Wall Street Journal* later labeled "the biggest shot in NBA history."

Example 5: Western Conference Semi Finals 2015 (Source: ESPN Stats and Information)

Game 1: Warriors 101, Grizzlies 86
(Warriors lead series 1–0; BPI gives Warriors 86 percent chance to win series)
Adjustments coming for Grizzlies defense? Will the Grizzlies change their defensive assignments in Game 2?
Klay Thompson was guarded by Tony Allen on eight of his eleven field goal attempts in the half-court offense in Game 1. Thompson shot five of eight (62.5 percent), with eleven points, when guarded by Allen, who limited opponents to 38.9 percent shooting in Round 1.

Game 2: Grizzlies 97, Warriors 90
(Series tied 1–1; BPI gives Warriors 69 percent chance to win series)
Tony Allen was seen yelling "First-Team All-Defense" repeatedly in the second half Tuesday. He may have proved his point (two weeks later he was selected to the NBA All-Defense First Team), limiting Warriors players to seven points on two-of-eleven shooting, and forcing three turnovers as the primary defender. He especially stymied Klay Thompson in half court:

Klay Thompson Half-Court Offense, Game 2 versus
Grizzlies

	vs Allen	vs all others
Points	2	9
Field goals	1 of 7	4 of 6
Turnovers	3	0

The bogusness: no adjustment made. Tony Allen simply
did what he does and made a better defensive commitment on
Thompson in Game 2 than in Game 1. Plus BPI didn't take
into consideration the return and impact of Michael Conley Jr.
in Game 2 after he missed Game 1 with a facial fracture.

Example 6: Real Plus/Minus versus Advanced Plus/Minus
versus Adjusted Plus/Minus versus Regularized Adjusted
Plus/Minus versus Box Plus/Minus versus "just" Plus/Minus.
The bogusness: just reread the header above.

The point here is that while analytics and advanced analytics
have their place in the game, don't refuse to take all things
into consideration or omit large parts of the facts in order to
validate your product. And throughout the implementation
of analytics in basketball, when it comes to insisting on its
importance, these omissions happen way too often, to the
extent that at times the omissions seem purposeful.

Just take the Philadelphia 76ers and their "process." Now
that the Sixers have become the new "it" team in the NBA,
former GM Sam Hinkie, respected by many as the "standard
bearer of the analytics movement," is credited for "the process"
he used in building the team, based partially on his use of analytics. To the point that it is whispered around the NBA that
he is a quasi–Billy Bean. All without addressing the reality that
he built the team through default methods, and had the Sixers
not dealt with back-to-back-to-back-to-back-to-back injuries
of every one of their high–first round selections from 2013 to
2018 (with the exceptions of Jahlil Okafor in 2016 and Michael

Carter-Williams in 2013, who ended up being the ROY they eventually traded), beginning with Nerlens Noel and continuing through the "almost season-ending" loss of Markelle Fultz, "the process" would have either looked totally different or not been a "process" at all.

It is the selling of the "brilliance" of that "process" that makes us paranoid when we ponder where "analyticals" will take the analytics movement and how disingenuous they will be in the efforts to make us fall in line with their beliefs and practices. Look, we all know that Joel Embiid getting healthy and Ben Simmons being drafted had nothing to do with analytics; the Sixers would just be perceived as larger damn fools than they already were, had they *not drafted* either of them. And keep in mind: had Embiid not gotten injured a second time, they probably would not have been in position even to draft Simmons because their record would have put them out of any real position to get another top-three draft pick. Same with Simmons, being injured his entire rookie season. Had that not happened—especially with his showing his true "generational value" by leading them to a number-three seed in the playoffs and winning ROY—they would not have been in lottery position to trade selections with Boston even to get Fultz with the first pick in the 2018 draft. Also, the signing of JJ Reddick had nothing to do with advanced metrics; that's just simple basketball, as it preaches court balance: Embiid, Jahlil Okafor (at the time), Dario Saric, Simmons, Robert Covington… *oh shit, we need somebody that can shoot from twenty feet and out on the regular, a three threat, we need someone to space the floor.* That's Basketball 101, not advanced trickle-down mathematics. Plus, entering the 2019–2020 season, the season "the process" is supposed to culminate with the Sixers finally reaching the NBA Finals, only two of the six major draft choices between 2013 and 2017, on which the original "process" was built, remain a part of the team. Yet, we are still being led to believe that the way it unfolded was all by design. Bo-gus-ness.

Understand, speaking truth to power is different from speaking power to half- or fragmented truths. But the people now running the game, in GM and EVP positions, as well as publishers, producers, editors, and storytellers in the business and media of sports (most with degrees or advanced degrees from elite schools such as Stanford, Harvard, or the University of Chicago, where NBA Commissioner Adam Silver, an analytics advocate, went to law school) are trying to impose the belief that *their* data is more true. They're hardly ever telling the whole story, continually leaving out parts to make *their* cases for applied analytics in basketball seem full proof and full truth, a further attempt to make us believe that *their* advanced knowledge and number-crunching experience in and of the game leads them—not us—to newer and greater conclusions. And those conclusions determine how teams are built, how players should be judged, how championships are won. Conclusions on how the game should now be played: Culture-*less*. Soul-*less*. Emotion-*less*. Numb.

It's the creation of a data utopia—*their* Wakanda—that strips away almost every layer of meaning the game has to us.

Paranoia is a muthafucka. A dark cloud hovering over the minds of men trapped in a society designed to suppress then steal their souls.

Or something like that. And in a capitalist society, where capitalist logic legislates behavior and "if it don't make money it don't make sense" becomes the sway of life, souls have a way of disappearing. As Quincy Jones once stated: "When you chase music for money, God walks out of the room." Just replace the word "music" with "sports" or any other creative activity, and "God" will more than likely do the same thing. Stage left.

Jim Novo, author of *Drilling Down: Turning Customer Data Into Profits with a Spreadsheet*, conceptualized analytics in this way, on his *Marketing Productivity* blog:

> Analytics bring accountability to people's work—often for the first time, they are being held directly accountable for their decisions... Accountability breeds fear—what if I am not doing the right thing? What if I am exposed as a "bad marketer" or a "bad designer"? Fear suppresses new ideas—this is of course the exact opposite of what you expect to happen; you expect that analysis will breed new ideas. But if this fear of accountability is not addressed, what happens is people recoil, they pull back, they want to go with the "tried and true" as opposed to experiment. As you can imagine, this is not helpful in a continuous improvement/testing scenario.

Breeds fear. Fear suppresses new ideas. So true. The same paranoia that black folks have of the police and of therapy is what some of us feel about analytics infiltrating "our" game. And the fear that it will turn the game into a function of "recoil," where the freedom to express ourselves is no longer central to the way we ball.

In a long-awaited piece written for *The Undefeated* in 2016, Michael Wilbon addressed the issue of black people, analytics, and basketball head on. In that article, former Phoenix Suns director of basketball operations and current ESPN basketball analyst/insider and show host Amin Elhassan connected the origin of the analytics movement in basketball to customer relations marketing in the auto industry, saying, "initially it was largely about data gathering." Well, the Tuskegee Experiment was data gathering, too.

Which brings me back to Barkley. And I'ma say what Barkley wouldn't say: there's a whole intrinsic and inherent racial dynamic that runs through the culture of analytics and basketball and the culture of basketball itself. It's the whole gatekeepers thing: "In order to enjoy your culture at the highest level, or to participate in it at a certain level, you will have to go through us." Yet it's subliminal. It's another example of black people's history in America repeating itself. And while some see it as basketball's advancement, some of us see it as basketball's new Jim Crow. Let's just call it Basketball Analytica.

Metric-based policing. About outcomes and not output. What people in general fail to understand or purposely forget is that sports—especially basketball—is more than just games for us. They've been a source of freedom. Basketball—and boxing, historically—have been the chief liberators. More than wins and losses, more than points, rebounds, assists, and ball movement, or what a team does per hundred possessions. Analytics when it comes to basketball, specifically the NBA, represents the counter to the game's culture. A culture that has been established over generations of black people finding ourselves through the game. The reducing it to numbers and data is the sterilization of the game. Numbers are necessary but unforgiving and unliberal. They handcuff creativity—or the advanced thought of it—like cops, on who else, black men. And who dominates the NBA? Don't lose sight of the analogy.

There's an old Richard Pryor joke that kinda sums up why this feeling exists:

> White guy: Why are you guys always holding your thangs?
> Black Guy: Because you motherfuckers done took everything else.

That's basketball to us. One of the few things in America we can hold on to and say with some misguided conviction that it is ours. The best similitude I can think of is a house. A house can either be a home or it can be property. For us basketball is a home; for analytics the game is property. That's how it seems, how it comes off from a "homeowner's" standpoint, how it *feels*.

In the words of Mark Twain (and so many others since): "There are three types of lies: Lies, damned lies, and statistics." We can argue forever about the fourth one. Look, at the end of the day analytics is dehumanizing and low-key racist. Schadenfreudish, too. It has the power to absolve the individuals in charge (be they owners, GMs, VPs of player ops, directors of strategy, innovation, and analytics, operation data scientists, system coordinators, or sabermetricians) of any responsibility when they trade a player, or when they sandbag or sabotage somebody's playing career. They can just point to "data" as though it is fate. Not *their* fate, someone else's.

One of the best comments on analytics came from Ben Alamar, the director of sports analytics for ESPN, when he said: "The data doesn't know who is actually playing." Which is kinda, sorta, maybe a little important when trying to revolutionize a sport, don't you think? Which is kinda, sorta, maybe somewhat important when the people who *are* playing are a part of the answer to the equations configured to determine games outcomes, how the game should be played, and how players are individually valued?

Analytics and "analyticals" don't see that. And to a degree, they aren't supposed to. That's not what they are in the game for. The game doesn't define their existence the way it does so many of ours. Their game is played on paper while the game itself isn't. Therein breeds the disconnect. Which is why some of us are so afraid of losing it. Afraid that in this moment and movement we are watching the game—our game—being slowly taken away. Stolen, like so many things in our history. Stolen, like us.

Which—in this very particular, specific, culturally biased case—makes paranoia a necessity.

CHAPTER 13

I (STILL) CAN'T BREATHE
Players versus Ownership versus Community and the Politics of Social Activism in American Professional Athletics

The question has forever been asked: *Do professional athletes have a responsibility outside of just being athletes*? Not that it will be answered in this book, but I hope a new way of looking at the question may result from asking it yet again.

It's no longer about being a role model, we're way beyond that. It's about being involved in society and the depth of that involvement; about being "woke," no longer "perfect." Which shifts the question to whether or not today's athletes have a responsibility to be involved in social issues. And, if so, in sports, are the athletes the only ones?

We hear it all the time: "It's not what name is on the back of the jersey, it's the name on the front that matters." Here is the funny thing about that saying: it's all good until something that really matters comes up. And when I say "matters," I mean beyond what happens on the field, court, pitch, or track, in the water, pit, octagon, or ring. I mean when sports takes a backseat to something different, when there's a call to speak up, out, or against. When those moments hit, for some strange reason, the names on the backs of jerseys seem to matter most.

And on the occasions when something goes wrong or situations get foul in the county, city, or community where a sports team is located, it's the players who are expected to say, do, or inspire. Calling on or calling out the organizations—the ones who put the name of the city, state, or country on the front of the jersey—almost never happens.

The social and societal responsibility in sports goes beyond the athletes. Yet almost all the *responsibility in sports,* as far as activism goes, falls to the athlete. George Zimmerman kills Trayvon Martin, an athlete is looked at to step forward; *Esquire* does a story on how activism has caught fire in the NBA, they put "LeBron Speaks" as the headline; an unjust war is started, the cameras and microphones seek and find an athlete to make public statement or take a public stand; unfair wage disparities for women, Venus Williams to the rescue.

And while all's fair in sports and protest, the lack of responsibility placed on others when it comes to matters of activism is concerning. Teams, organizations, owners, and executives are hardly ever demanded to play roles in movements where the mission is to institute change. Society would rather hear from Cristiano Ronaldo than Juventus about the plight of his people the same way it looked to Roberto Clemente to learn about the plight of his.

I'm not saying it never happens, just that an individual's fame should not be the determining factor in who is expected to save or change situations. Players have popularity, but teams and owners have resources and connections and followings

that are more unconditional and generational and longer last-
ing than most players. Add to that: teams (for the most part)
don't move. Their roots run deep in the places they play. They
stay longer and exist longer than any player ever has. Just ask
the Yankees. Which, as an organization, is more New York
than Ruth, DiMaggio, Maris, Yogi, Reggie, Jeter, Rivera,
Martin, and Steinbrenner combined. And the Yankees organization has more power.

In 1993 the staff at *Newsweek*, in an essay on athlete responsibility titled "I'm Not A Role Model," wrote this: "Celebrities
like [Charles] Barkley may decline the honor, but their high
visibility obliges them to behave with at least an awareness that
they are being watched by millions. Like it or not, they have
a power of influence on worshipful young fans multiplied by
the huge factor of television—perhaps even more so among the
minority poor, who have few other avatars of success to excite
their hopes."

Why can't the same be said about the teams for which these
athletes play? The teams remain in the community while players throughout their careers are traded and are often no longer
directly connected to the areas where the need remains. Not
saying that teams and organizations do nothing, but the public
expectation of them is not the same as it is of the athlete. When,
plain and simple, *it should be*. The single-mindedness of both
media and fans let organizations off the hook.

The pressure is undue and unbalanced, the responsibility
unequal and unshared. The questions of "Should athletes be
role models?" and "Do athletes have responsibilities beyond
being athletes?" are flawed. Wrecked. Drew Brees and Anthony
Davis should not have more pressure on them to do things in
and for New Orleans than the Saints and the Pelicans organizations. Steph Curry shouldn't have more responsibility in the
Bay than the Warriors or the ownership group that purchased

the team in 2010. Alexander Ovechkin, John Wall, and Bryce Harper shouldn't be looked to step up concerning public social issues in the DC area if the Capitols, Wizards, and Nationals aren't. Same with Jose Altuve and JJ Watt in Houston; Brianna Stewart and Russell Wilson in Seattle. Even in the cases of an individual superstar, the franchises and owners of the franchises in which the athlete's sport operates carry the same weight as the individual who keeps that sport in the national or international spotlight, while having resources and power far beyond than that of a single athlete.

Point: just because Michael Jordan is black—and a former player—doesn't mean he's allowed to be singled out as the only owner the media and public demand take a stand on something that directly affects the people who invest in their teams. Social issues are universal, even as they impact specific groups of people. Fandom doesn't discriminate, for the most part. Especially when it comes to fairness and death. Women owners and women's sports teams should not be the only ones fighting for issues that affect fair and civil treatment of women; black owners and sports that have a large population of black and nonwhite athletes should not be the only ones protesting for issues that affect fairness and civility toward people of color.

In a piece entitled "Black NFL Players Should Exert Their Power," written for the *Washington Post* by Shaun Harper, a USC professor and executive director of the USC Race and Equality Center, waxes journalistic on the continual view of black men in sports solely as "laborers and entertainers." Although Harper's piece is on point, the problem rests with the title (which might have been written by an editor). It shouldn't be just "black NFL players" who are called on to exert their power. Especially when the teams the "black players" play for collectively carry more power than the black players ever will.

It is utopian in thought and, on the surface, unrealistic to harbor any great expectations, but it is worth opening a discussion and paying attention. A simple, "Well, I see Carmelo Anthony out here in Baltimore in the streets with the people protesting—what are the Ravens and Orioles doing, as teams that represent the city of Baltimore?" would be a start. Because, as I said earlier, the names on the backs of the jerseys change, but the ones on the front are usually here to stay. It's facing the truth about who really has the juice—the individual or the organization? The athlete or the owner? The player or the game?

"The Andersons got tickets to the game? How'd they get tickets?" The Andersons got tickets because they knew someone. The Andersons got tickets because they are plugged and privileged. The Andersons got tickets because they could afford season tickets. The Andersons got tickets because they have disposable income in a way that most don't. The Andersons got tickets because Dad used to work for the league. The Andersons got tickets because Mom sits on the team's board. The Anderson got tickets because their kids are on a first-name basis with all the players on the team. The Andersons got tickets because the senior VP of sales went to Stanford with Mr. Anderson. The Andersons got tickets because their daughter is engaged to a player. The Andersons got tickets because they've hosted "friends of" parties at their home for the team. The Andersons got tickets because they've donated more time and money to the team's charities than any family in the state. The Andersons got tickets because their family helped get the new stadium built. The Andersons got tickets because Mr. Anderson's brother sits on the city's urban planning council. The Andersons got ticket because their youngest son is being groomed to one day run for mayor. The Andersons got tickets because Grandpa Anderson has a street in town named after him. The Andersons got tickets because their family represents everything the organization wants fans of the organization to represent… and look like. The Andersons got tickets because the Andersons make shit happen. The Andersons got tickets because the Andersons are *those* people.

If sports is supposed to be universal, if it is supposed to be this nation's—or the world's—equalizer, normalizer, the thing that is *supposed* to override anything while overlooking everything, the thing that brings us all together through the power of itself, then why are we here? Why are digital and broadcast programs built on debate and argument, constructing an entire radio and internet culture using sports as the divide, cultivating a sports world in which opposites (opinions, feelings, beliefs) do anything but attract? Why are collective bargaining agreements historically so contentious that league shutdowns aren't abnormal? Why does it seem that the disconnect between management and labor (owners and players) gets wider each decade? Why is there so much public resentment of athletes exercising more power and control of their careers? Because sports is not just sports. It is not a game. Hardly ever has been. Let's no longer fool ourselves into believing sports is just a form of athletic entertainment, that it is a "privilege" for those who participate in it and get paid for it at the highest level. We can no longer be that naive, no longer be *those* people.

The fundamental concept of affording equal chance and opportunity through various forms of athletic competition is noble and can be used as an example of how society *should* function. But while sports at its core has the power to be what it wants to be, it's the businesspeople who control sports who choose a different route.

Still waiting to see a commissioner of color run one of the professional leagues.

Still wanting the Rooney Rule to *not* be necessary.

Still hoping one day an ownership group reflects the audience it serves.

Still fighting for women to experience leverage and equality in and through sports.

Still the number of African Americans in MLB is appalling.

Still Kaepernick ain't playing.

Still told (and widely expected) to "shut up and dribble."

Still 85 percent of the sports editors, 77 percent of the assistant sports editors, 82 percent of the sports reporters, 80 percent of the sports columnists, 78 percent of copy editors and designers in the business of print and digital sports media are white. And over 82 percent are white and male.

Still an extremely low percentage of minority and women athletic directors in the NCAA.

Still LeBron James gets "nigger" spray-painted on the front gate of his house.

Still we wait to breathe in sports, with the belief that in America sports gives many of us our best chance to exhale. Sports historically has been a pulpit for protest. From Jack Johnson (boxing) denouncing white supremacy and speaking out against racist American attitudes in Mexico to Arthur Ashe (tennis) fighting against apartheid in South Africa and for affirmative action in America to Carlos Delgado (MLB) and Steve Nash (NBA) openly protesting the Iraq War, sports has been the vehicle by which many voices have been heard, many minds changed, many ideologies adjusted, many generations altered in thought.

Still.

So often those protests have been individual, hardly ever collective. America has done a somewhat masterful and, more than likely, calculated job of reducing protest in sports so that it looks singular at best, minimal at worst. The "black fist" image of John Carlos and Tommie Smith at the 1968 Olympics has basically become the sports equivalent of the "I Have a Dream" speech for a reality that is so much bigger. Leading us—an often apathetic audience and society—to think and believe historically on the surface that *that's* all there was; that an entire fight, cause, movement was represented in that *one moment*. Statement was made, everybody got it. Thank you, next.

And even in the subtext of the moment, there is selectivity in who will be the face of the movement. See, no one wants to admit this, but Derrick Rose wore the "I Can't Breathe" shirt first. LeBron James gets the credit, but truth be told, Rose donned the iconic T-shirt a game before. Sort of how Claudette Colvin refused to give up her seat at the front of the bus before Rosa Parks. But Derrick Rose ain't LeBron James. Being LeBron carries much more weight and messages go further with him attached. And that, too, is the power and politics of the game. Everybody plays while getting played.

Now it's Kaepernick's afro'd, kneeling silhouette that is the symbol. The reduction. No inclusion of the others—the Michael Bennetts, the Steph Currys, the Gregg Popovichs, the Steve Kerrs, the Eric Reeds, the WNBA collective, the Carmelo Anthonys, the Chris Longs and Adam Joneses, the Gabby Douglasses and Aly Raismans, the Adam Silvers. On the surface of public perception, they don't exist. And when their presence is felt or heard, they're afterthoughts. Secondary civil rights citizens. Custodians of virtue. Influencers. It's all the same. Anything to give the overall and future impression that those in sports who fight for rights, fight alone.

When protest meets power meets politics meets sports: we've seen them all come together—or collide, depending on your POV—each time providing a different outcome. What outcome will this latest "collision" render? (The NBA/China fallout notwithstanding.) Given the state America is in, the divided mindset of the people, the players' struggles and maneuvers for power, the refusal to relinquish position or provide leverage by those in power, the current outcome may not be an outcome at all—with sports transforming into something much more than a game, athletes subscribing to be much more than just athletes, and fans believing more and more that we have earned the right to be more than just fans.

Recent incidents that run counter to the narrative and tone of this chapter are important to include here. When Stephon Clarke was shot and killed by members of the Sacramento Police Department in March 2018, not only did the Sacramento Kings organization make a public statement in support of Clarke, they put mouth and money to it by partnering with the Build. Black. coalition and Black Lives Matter. Stephen Ross, owner of the Miami Dolphins, and Robert Sarver, owner of the Phoenix Suns, have been at the forefront of outspokenness on social and civil justice issues in the past. And while Detroit Lions defensive end Ezekiel Ansah and other members of the team got the attention for donating around a hundred thousand bottles of water to families during the Flint, Michigan, water crisis and other area-connected athletes from Rasheed Wallace to Kyle Kuzma lent both time, money, and voice, it was the Pistons' owner, Tom Gores, who not only granted $1 million of his pledge to the FlintNow relief fund but also spearheaded an initiative to raise $10 million from other private businesses to donate to the crisis.

While this type of public involvement by teams and owners in situations that directly impact and involve black and brown people isn't on the regular, it also isn't obsolete. And needs to be acknowledged. But just as there are some (millions) who will claim it is not the responsibility of the team or organization to get involved in such things, in truth, neither is it the players'. But that somehow always gets lost in translation. As does the stark difference between labor and ownership across the landscape of sports, the constant reminder of the race factor at play in this translation loss. This is (still) America.

Much as the election of Donald Trump may have forced the Gen Y and Z generations to become politically active, the same may be said about his election and its impact on sports. For years the quiet discussion about how athletes weren't what they used to be has eaten away at the true potential sports had to wield its power in American society. "Athletes aren't built like they used to be. Strong arms and legs, weak spines." Those were the careless whispers. And while small, incremental changes were beginning to surface before Trump's political entrance, the true ambition and power of sports didn't begin to manifest until after he took his oath of office. Sports pushed the light-speed button, fast-tracking back to an era when athletes were among the county's loudest voices.

And even though there seems to be a necessarily uncomfortable level of discourse and understanding between the White House and so many current athletes who didn't vote for Trump (and the owners and gatekeepers in sports who did), his election, at least, made every athlete born after 1980 know that some shit like this *can* happen. Trump gave the American sports world the wake-up call it needed.

Sports by nature is about reaction. It is about how an athlete responds to an immediate stimulus. In the moment. Off the fields of dreams, the same facts hold. Sports reacts to both times and circumstance, reality and dreams. A league full of David Wests would be a beautiful thing, but a non-reality. A game full of Megan Rapinoes would be an even more beautiful thing, but also a non-reality. A country full of Bennetts and Bileses, Kerrs and Currys, would be too beautiful a thing. But... we all know. As Gregg Popovich has always said to players about America: "You've got to understand where we live."

Sports has the power to be our reminder. It is hard to breathe when the game's foot is on your neck. When all the social responsibility is on you to be model and savior. It's the sports version of the graphene-splitting difference between "Life is what you make it" and "Life is what you *are allowed* to make it."

Nelson Mandela believed that the power of sports could "change the world." His exact words: "Sports has the power to change the world. It has the power to inspire. It has the power to unite people in a way that little else does. It speaks to youth in a way they understand. Sport can create hope when there once was only despair." *Preach.* This from a boxer who, much like Ali, fought in and out of the ring. *Yet.* No disrespect, but when Madiba was speaking about the power of sports he most definitely wasn't thinking about the power of the people *who run sports*. He left that for the rest of us to figure out.

EPILOGUE
Eddie

Below is a great example of the ways in which racism, the subtle politics of the game, and the power of media to dictate the narrative in sports interact—and why there was a small necessity for this book to be written.

This was published December 8, 2016, on cleverst.com, in an article titled "College Football's BEST Coaches of All Time!" Here's what they wrote:

Eddie Robinson

Robinson might be a controversial choice on our list but we'll keep him in, anyway. Robinson spent 56 years coaching at Grambling State where he would lead over 200 players to the NFL. Robinson won 408 games in his career, making him the winningest coach in the game.

Seriously. And it don't, won't, ever... stop.

SOURCES

Introduction

The Wire, "Game Day," HBO, August 4, 2002, https://www.youtube.com/watch?v=VJrHpAUfnk0.

Kareem Abdul-Jabbar, "What Sports Taught Me About America," *Guardian*, August 28, 2018, https://www.theguardian.com/sport/2018/aug/28/notes-from-an-ungrateful-athlete-why-race-and-sports-matter-in-america.

Quoted in Shaun King, "Dear White People: Be More Like Gregg Popovich," *Intercept*, October 17, 2017, https://theintercept.com/2017/10/17/gregg-popovich-trump-white-privledge-race-kaepernick/.

Rembert Browne, "Spike Lee Wants You To Wake Up," *Time*, August 20, 2018.

Quoted by Laura Ingraham, "The Ingraham Angle," Fox News, February 16, 2018, https://www.youtube.com/watch?v=fJlA2lkpXsw.

Quoted by Odell Beckham Jr., *The Shop*, "Episode 1," HBO, August 28, 2018, https://www.hbo.com/the-shop/episodes/episode-1.

Public Enemy, "He Got Game" (Def Jam Records, released May 2, 1998) https://www.youtube.com/watch?v=7FmPskTljo0.

Chapter 1

Quoted in Seth Wickersham and Don Van Natta Jr., "NFL Owners Struggled To Retain Control Under Trump's Attacks, Rise of Player Protest," ESPN.com, October 1, 2017, http://www.espn.com/espn/otl/story/_/id/20865444/inside-story-happened-players-took-control-nfl-national-anthem.

Quoted in ESPN News Services, wire story, ESPN.com, September 19, 2018, http://www.espn.com/nfl/story/_/id/24720441/group-hall-famers-threaten-boycott-induction-ceremony-nfl-provides-health-insurance-annual-salaries.

Ted C. Fishman, "The Football Helmet of the Future," *Chicago Magazine*, December 18, 2017, https://www.chicagomag.com/Chicago-Magazine/January-2018/Riddell-Football-Helmets-InSite/.

Scoop Jackson, "The Rooney Rule Bamboozle-Move," *The Shadow League,* January 26, 2013, https://theshadowleague.com/tsl-op-ed-th

e-rooney-rule-bamboozle-move/.

Wayne Allyn Root, "The Suicide of the NFL," Townhall.com, September 27, 2017, https://townhall.com/columnists/wayneallynroot /2017/09/27/the-suicide-of-the-nfl-n2387019.

Mase, "Feels So Good" (Bad Boy Records, released October 14, 1997), https://www.youtube.com/watch?v=rIvEiTrq9kk.

Karen Casteel, "How Do Americans Feel about the Protests? It Depends on How You Ask," FiveThirtyEight.com, October 9, 2017, https:// fivethirtyeight.com/features/how-do-americans-feel-about-the-nfl -protests-it-depends-on-how-you-ask.

Quoted in Alex Altman and Sean Gregory, "Why He Always Bounces Back," *Time*, October 9, 2017, http://time.com/4960638/donald -trump-latest-battle-against-nfl/.

Quoted on Jake Tapper's *The Lead*, interview, CNN, September 25, 2017, https://www.cnn.com/videos/tv/2017/09/25/doug-baldwin -protest-live-jake-tapper.cnn.

Quoted in *West Virginia State Board of Education v. Burnette*, Justice Robert Jackson, Supreme Court ruling, June 14, 1943, https://www.oyez.org /cases/1940-1955/319us624; Quoted in Donald Scarinci, "1943 Ruling Offers Insight on National Anthem Controversy," *Observer*, November 23, 2017, https://observer.com/2017/11/1943-court-ruling -offers-insight-on-national-anthem-controversy/.

Jeffery Frank, "Trump and the Art of Irrational Provocation," *New Yorker*, October 4, 2017, https://www.newyorker.com/news/daily -comment/trump-and-the-art-of-irrational-provocation.

Quoted on *First Take*, interview, ESPN, January 9, 2018.

Quoted by Dale Earnhardt, @DaleJr, Twitter, September 25, 2017.

Chapter 2

Quoted in "Unlimited" series, Nike, Widen + Kennedy, ad campaign, September 2016, https://www.adweek.com/creativity/nike-calls -serena-williams-greatest-athlete-ever-striking-us-open-ad-173254/.

Scoop Jackson, "Equal Rights in Sports," ESPN.com, July 20, 2007, http://www.espn.com/espn/page2/story?page=jackson/070719.

Quoted in Stephanie Zacharek, "Women's Rage Is the Most Powerful Engine in 2018," *Time*, September 24, 2018, http://time.com /5404884/women-anger-politics-2018/.

Nicki Lisa Cole, "Understanding the Sociological Perspective: How Sociologists See the World," ThoughtCo.com, July 2, 2018, https://www.thoughtco.com/sociological-perspective-3026642.

"A Timeline of Social Activism in Sports," photo gallery, CNN, January 9, 2018, https://www.cnn.com/2016/12/12/sport/gallery/social -activism-in-sports/index.html.

Dee Dee Meyers, *Why Women Should Rule the World* (New York: Harper Collins, 2008), 81.

Devereaux Peters, "I've Won Two WNBA Championships. Men Need to Stop Challenging Me to Play One-on-One," *Lily,* August 4, 2018, https://www.thelily.com/ive-won-two-wnba-championships-men-need-to-stop-challenging-me-to-play-one-on-one/.

Quoted by Natalie Weiner, @natalieweiner, Twitter, November 19, 2018.

Stephen Curry, "This Is Personal," *Players Tribune,* August 26, 2018, https://www.theplayerstribune.com/en-us/articles/stephen-curry-womens-equality.

Kurt Badenhausen, "Why No Women Rank in the World's 100 Highest-Paid Athletes," *Forbes,* July 7, 2018, https://www.forbes.com/sites/kurtbadenhausen/2018/06/07/why-no-women-ranked-among-the-worlds-100-highest-paid-athletes/#a1ffdc93479b.

"World's Highest-Paid Athletes: The List," *Forbes,* 2018, https://www.forbes.com/athletes/#3c12b82255ae.

Quoted in Maggie Mertens, "World Cup 2015: Women's Soccer Is a Feminist Issue," *Atlantic,* June 5, 2015, https://www.theatlantic.com/entertainment/archive/2015/06/womens-soccer-is-a-feminist-issue/394865.

Dan Szczepanek, "Ranking the Nine Best (and Only) Female Owners in Sports, GrandstandCentral.com, January 28, 2018, https://grandstandcentral.com/2018/sections/gender/best-women-owners-sports/.

Des Bieler, "After Saying Girls 'Pretty Much Ruin Everything,' High School AD Placed on Leave," *Washington Post,* September 27, 2018, https://www.washingtonpost.com/sports/2018/09/27/high-school-ad-placed-leave-after-saying-girls-pretty-much-ruin-everything/?utm_term=.4479f58ddc5a.

Tucker Center for Research on Women and Girls in Sport, *Media Coverage & Female Athletes,* video documentary, University of Minnesota, 2014, https://www.cehd.umn.edu/tuckercenter/projects/mediacoverage.html.

Kayla Lombardo, "SI Sportsperson of The Year: A History of Female Winners," *Sports Illustrated,* December 9, 2015, https://www.si.com/si-sportsperson-history-female-winners-serena-williams.

Stephen R. Covey, *The 7 Habits Of Highly Effective People: Personal Lessons in Personal Change* (New York: Free Press, 2004), 241.

Chapter 3

Anthony Slater, "Why Warriors Coach Steve Kerr Speaks Out on Social Issues," San Jose *Mercury News,* February 17, 2017, https://www.mercurynews.com/2017/02/17/steve-kerr-explains-his-willingness-to-speak-out-amidst-a-coaching-profession-where-others-remain-quiet.

Anthony Slater, "Warriors coach Steve Kerr Advocates Non-Violent Protest," San Jose *Mercury News,* September 21, 2016, https://www

.mercurynews.com/2016/09/21/warriors-coach-steve-kerr-advocates
-non-violent-protests-says-hes-comfortable-with-social-activism
-from-his-players.

Charlotte Carroll, "Phil Jackson, Steve Kerr Discuss How the NBA
Handles Social and Political Issues," *Sports Illustrated*, September
19, 2018, https://www.si.com/nba/2018/09/19/phil-jackson-steve
-kerr-discuss-social-issues.

Marc J. Spears, "Gregg Popovich Is the NBA's Most 'Woke' Coach," *The
Undefeated*, November 9, 2016, http://theundefeated.com/features
/san-antonio-spurs-gregg-popovich-is-the-nbas-most-woke-coach.

Greg Logan, "Spurs Coach Gregg Popovich Addresses Social Issues before
Game," *Newsday*, January 17, 2018, https://www.newsday.com/sports
/basketball/nets/spurs-gregg-popovich-social-issues-1.16233344.

Spears, "Gregg Popovich Is The NBA's Most 'Woke' Coach."

Jeremy Bergman, "Doug Pederson Would Join Eagles in Teamwide Ges-
ture," NFL.com, September 17, 2016, http://www.nfl.com/news
/story/0ap3000000703966/article/doug-pederson-would-join-eagles
-in-teamwide-gesture.

Kyle Korver, "Privileged," *Players Tribune*, April 8, 2019, https://www
.theplayerstribune.com/en-us/articles/kyle-korver-utah-jazz-nba.

James Doubek, "'We Don't Have Enough Women in Power': Notre Dame
Coach Muffet McGraw Goes Viral," NPR, April 6, 2019, https://
www.npr.org/2019/04/06/710539614/we-don-t-have-enough
-women-in-power-notre-dame-coach-muffet-mcgraw-goes-viral.

Alex Pappademas, "The Political Avenger: Chris Evans Takes on Trump,
Tom Brady, Anxiety, and Those Retirement Rumors," *Hollywood
Reporter*, March 27, 2019, https://www.hollywoodreporter.com
/features/chris-evans-talks-trump-tom-brady-anxiety-retirement
-rumors-1196705.

Carron J. Phillips, "When White Athletes Use Their Privilege for Good,"
New York Daily News, August 1, 2017, https://www.nydailynews
.com/sports/white-athletes-privilege-good-article-1.3374300.

Chapter 4

Quoted in *Forbes* Under 30 Summit, interview, October 4, 2017; Quoted
in "Kendrick Lamar Praises Colin Kaepernick," *Highsnobiety*, October
5, 2017.

Quoted in "Dream Crazy," Nike, ad campaign, September 2018;
https://abcnews.go.com/Business/nike-sales-booming
-kaepernick-ad-invalidating-critics/story?id=59957137.

Quoted in Dilab Tyseer, @dilab_tyseer, Twitter, December 5, 2017; quoted
in MichelleObama'sSideEye, @A_Nese_ssary, Twitter, December
6, 2017; quoted in Govfella, @govfella, Twitter, December 6, 2017,
quoted in GeauxVols, @kwessner1, Twitter, December 6, 2017.

Quoted in Logan Murdock, "Kevin Durant's Epiphany About Being Black

In America," San Jose *Mercury News*, November 27, 2017, https://www.mercurynews.com/2017/11/27/exclusive-kevin -durants-epiphany-about-being-black-in-america/.

Quoted in "The Making of Colin Kaepernick," *Washington Post,* September 7, 2017, https://www.washingtonpost.com/sports/the -making-of-colin-kaepernick/2017/09/07/d4d58e20-9320-11e7 -8754-d478688d23b4_story.html?noredirect=on&utm_term =.1cd799c0b78a.

Quoted in "Roland Martin Goes Off on Bill O'Reilly over Colin Kaepernick Critique," *Wrap*, September 16, 2016, https://www.thewrap .com/roland-martin-bill-oreilly-colin-kaepernick-tv-one-fox-news -national-anthem/.

Cathy Burke, "Fox's O'Reilly: Kaepernick 'Overhyped' Issue, Created 'Hostility,'" *Newsmax*, September 13, 2016, https://www.newsmax .com/US/Kaepernick-brutality-police-protest/2016/09/13/id/748136.

Laura Bradley, "Is Netflix About to Steal Kenya Barris from ABC?" *Vanity Fair*, April 4, 2018, https://www.vanityfair.com/hollywood/2018/04 /kenya-barris-leaving-abc-netflix-black-ish.

Lowell Cohn, "49ers' Colin Kaepernick Ignores the Contradiction of His Outrage," *Press Democrat*, August 28, 2016, https://www .pressdemocrat.com/sports/6024734-181/lowell-cohn-kaepernick -ignores-the.

Lowell Cohn, "A Humble Suggestion for 49ers' Colin Kaepernick," *Press Democrat*, October 7, 2015. https://www.pressdemocrat.com /sports/4585250-181/lowell-cohn-a-humble-suggestion.

Darren Rovell, "Poll: Niners QB Colin Kaepernick Most Disliked Player in League," ESPN.com, September 22, 2016, http://www.espn.com /nfl/story/_/id/17604958/san-francisco-49ers-qb-colin-kaepernick- most-disliked-player-nfl-according-poll-e-poll-marketing-research.

2016 NFL Approximate Value Released, Footballperspective.com, http:// www.footballperspective.com/2016-approximate-value-released.

2016 NFL Passing, Statistics, ProFootballReferences.com, https://www .pro-football-reference.com/years/2016/passing.htm.

2017 NFL Passing, Statistics, ProFootballReferences.com, https://www .pro-football-reference.com/players/K/KeenCa00.htm.

Reuben Fischer-Baum, Neil Greenberg, and Mike Hume, "The Colin Kaepernick Tracker," *Washington Post*, September 7, 2017, https:// www.washingtonpost.com/graphics/2017/sports/kaepernick-tracker/.

2017 NFL Passing, Statistics, ProFootballReferences.com, https://www .pro-football-reference.com/years/2017/passing.htm.

Robert O'Connell, "The NFL Is Making Colin Kaepernick's Collusion Case For Him," *Atlantic*, November 15, 2017, https://www .theatlantic.com/entertainment/archive/2017/11/the-nfl-is-making -colin-kaepernicks-collusion-case-for-him/545804.

Michael McCann, "Why The Arbitrator Rules In Favor of Colin Kaepernick, and What This Means for the NFL," *Sports Illustrated*, August 30, 2018, https://www.si.com/nfl/2018/08/30/colin-kaepernick -collusion-case-nfl-arbitrator.

Brady Henderson, "Michael Bennett Says Colin Kaepernick Resolution Needed Before More Talks With Owners," ESPN.com, October 19, 2017, http://www.espn.com/nfl/story/_/id/21069553/michael -bennett-seattle-seahawks-says-job-colin-kaepernick-first-step -moving-ahead-owners.

Vann R. Newkirk, "No Country For Colin Kaepernick," *Atlantic*, August 11, 2017, https://www.theatlantic.com/entertainment /archive/2017/08/no-country-for-colin-kaepernick/536340.

Jerry Brewer, "Sorry for the Inconvenience Fans, but Black Athlete Activism Is Multiplying," *Washington Post*, August 16, 2017, https:// www.washingtonpost.com/sports/sorry-for-the-inconvenience -fans-but-black-athlete-activism-is-multiplying/2017/08/16/.

Stevie Wonder, *Black Man* (Crystal Sound, released September 1976).

Chapter 5

Spike Lee dir., *Do The Right Thing*, Universal Pictures, 1989.

Des Bieler, "Dick Vitale, NBA Coach Rip Lavar Ball, ESPN, but Lakers Coach Luke Walton Cracks a Joke," *Washington Post*, https://www .washingtonpost.com/news/early-lead/wp/2018/01/07/dick-vitale -rips-lavar-ball-and-espn-after-latest-shots-at-lakers-coaching/?utm _term=.c4852f69a2f5.

Quoted on *First Things First*, FOX Sports, May 2, 2018, https://www .foxsports.com/watch/first-things-first/video/1175027267529.

Monica Lewinsky, "Emerging from 'The House of Gaslight' in the Age of #METOO," *Vanity Fair*, February 25, 2018, https://www .vanityfair.com/news/2018/02/monica-lewinsky-in-the-age-of -metoo.

Kent Babb, "Practiced Patience," *Washington Post,* June 14, 2018, https://www.washingtonpost.com/news/sports/wp/2018/06/14 /feature/lavar-balls-wifes-quiet-recovery/?utm_term=.696b683130a1.

Chapter 6

Quoted in "LeBron James Thinks His Greatness 'Gets Taken for Granted at Times,'" Slamonline, December 6, 2017, https://www .slamonline.com/archives/lebron-james-greatness-taken-for-granted.

Stefan Fatsis, "'No Viet Cong Ever Called Me Nigger': The Story Behind the Famous Quote That Muhammad Ali Probably Never Said," Slate.com, June 8, 2016, https://slate.com/culture/2016/06/did -muhammad-ali-ever-say-no-viet-cong-ever-called-me-nigger.html.

Laura Wagner, "'Republicans Buy Sneakers Too': That Quote Has Haunted Michael Jordan for Decades. But Did He Really Say It?" Slate.com, July 28, 2016, https://slate.com/culture/2016/07/did

-michael-jordan-really-say-republicans-buy-sneakers-too.html.

Quoted in Jeremiah Short, "LeBron James Stop Crying, Bro,"
locker-report.com, March 25, 2016, https://locker-report.com
/lebron-james-stop-crying-bro.

Ben Golliver, "NBA Announces Record Salary Cap for 2016–17 after Historic Climb," *Sports Illustrated*, July 2, 2016, https://www.si.com
/nba/2016/07/02/nba-salary-cap-record-numbers-2016-adam-silver.

Chris Broussard and Brian Windhorst, "Tristan Thompson Resigns with
Cavaliers for 5 Years, $82 Million," ESPN.com, October 22, 2015,
http://www.espn.com/nba/story/_/id/13942794/cleveland-cavaliers
-tristan-thompson-agree-5-year-82-million-deal.

Quoted by Alex Heimann on Quora, May 2018.

Quoted in "Legendary Hoops Writer, Scoop Jackson, Talks NBA Finals
Predictions, Jordan vs. LeBron, Chicago Hip-Hop and More," Hype-
beast.com, May 31, 2017, https://hypebeast.com/2017/5
/scoop-jackson-interview-essentials-2017-nba-finals-predictions
-michael-jordan-versus-lebron-james-chicago-hip-hop.

"Jordan-LeBron Debate Tackled by Harvard and Yale," ESPN, June 10,
2018, http://www.espn.com/video/clip/_/id/23753065.

"LeBron James Walks Out of Game 1 Press Conference after Question
about J. R. Smith Blunder," video, *ESPN*, May 31, 2018, https://www.
youtube.com/watch?v=Tk_EBNLyqxw; "LeBron James Wears Hand
Cast in Postgame Press Conference after Game 4, Explains Injury,"
video, ESPN, June 9, 2018, https://www.youtube.com
/watch?v=3cLeyrS1cW8.

David French, "Yes, LeBron James Is the GOAT," *National Review*, May
31, 2018, https://www.nationalreview.com/2018/05/lebron-james
-goat/#slide-1.

Dan Wolken, "Now Is the Perfect Time to Have the LeBron James vs.
Michael Jordan GOAT Debate," *USA Today*, May 29, 2018,
https://www.usatoday.com/story/sports/2018/05/29/michael-jordan
-lebron-james-its-time-have-goat-debate/650313002.

Quoted from "LeBron James Sits Down with Rachel Nichols to Discuss
9th NBA Finals Trip," interview, ESPN, May 31, 2018, https://www
.slamonline.com/slam-tv/lebron-james-asked-cavs-not-trade-kyrie
-irving.

Terry Pluto, "LeBron James: No Matter Where He Goes, Same Problems
Loom," *Cleveland Plain Dealer*, June 29, 2018, https://www.cleveland.com
/pluto/index.ssf/2018/06/lebron_james_no_matter_where_h.html.

Chapter 7

Allison Kilkenny, "Philadelphia Private Swim Club Forces out Black Children," *Huffington Post*, May 25, 2011, https://www.huffpost.com
/entry/philadelphia-private-swim_b_228253.

Lauren DiSanto, "Settlement in Swim Club Discrimination

Case," NBCPhiladelphia.com, August 16, 2012, https://www
.nbcphiladelphia.com/news/national-international/settlement
-in-swim-club-discrimination-case/1938088.

Chapter 8
Sandra Garcia, "Jemele Hill Is Joining *Atlantic* and Is Ready to Talk Politics," *New York Times*, October 1, 2018, https://www.nytimes
.com/2018/10/01/sports/jemele-hill-the-atlantic-.html.

Chapter 10
Lawrence D. Hogan, *Shades of Glory: The Negro League and the Story
of African American Baseball* (New York: Penguin Random House,
2007), 263.
Richard Justice, "'Selig Rule' First of Its Kind in Sports," MLB.com,
August 26, 2013, https://www.mlb.com/news/richard-justice
-selig-rule-first-of-its-kind-in-sports/c-58500104.
Dave Zirin, *Welcome to the Terrordome: The Pain, Politics, and Promise of
Sports* (Chicago: Haymarket Books, 2007), 171
Mark Armour and Daniel R. Levitt, "Baseball Demographics, 1947–
2016," Society for American Baseball Research, undated, https://sabr
.org/bioproj/topic/baseball-demographics-1947-2012.
Associated Press, "MLB Says Percentage of Black Players Highest since
2012," *USA Today*, April 10, 2018, https://www.usatoday.com/story
/sports/mlb/2018/04/10/mlb-says-percentage-of-black-players
-highest-since-2012/33696133.
Bill Shaikin, "Major League Baseball Is 'Failing' in Its Attempt to Increase
Front Office Diversity and the Issue Could Get Worse," *Los Angeles
Times*, June 30, 2017, https://www.latimes.com/sports/mlb
/la-sp-baseball-diversity-minority-hiring-20170630-story.html.
Hogan, *Shades of Glory,* 376
Armour and Levitt, "Baseball Demographics, 1947–2016."
Chris Isidore, "Green Behind Decline of Blacks in Baseball," CNN Money,
April 13, 2007, https://money.cnn.com/2007/04/13/commentary
/sportsbiz/index.htm.
Branson Wright, "Urban Youth Academies Get Black Players Back in the
Game," *The Undefeated*, July 7, 2017, https://theundefeated.com
/features/urban-youth-baseball-academies-cincinnati.

See also the following:
Anthony Witrado, "How Tim Anderson Is Becoming Baseball's Savior," *Forbes*, April 30, 2019, https://www.forbes.com/sites
/anthonywitrado/2019/04/30/how-tim-anderson-is-becoming
-baseballs-savior/#d1e866c55499.
Scoop Jackson, "Eleven Weeks of Irrelevance," ESPN.com, July 13,
2007, http://www.espn.com/espn/page2/story?page=jackson/070712.

Leigh Steinberg, "Why Have African American Players Disappeared in MLB?" *Forbes*, April 17, 2018, https://www.forbes.com/sites /leighsteinberg/2018/04/17/why-have-african-american-players -disappeared-in-mlb/#4dee230450df.

Chapter 11

Sandra J. Ball-Rokeach and Melvin L. DeFleur, "A Dependency Model of Mass-Media Effects," *Communication Research* 3, no. 1 (January 1976): 3–21.

Cork Gaines, "Tiger Woods Has Climbed 1,186 Spots in the World Golf Rankings in Less Than a Year," *Business Insider,* September 24, 2018, https://www.businessinsider.com/tiger-woods-world-golf-ranking -2018-9.

Wikipedia, "Roger Federer," https://en.wikipedia.org/wiki/Roger_Federer.

Mika Honkasalo, "How the Warriors Got Kevin Durant and What It Means for the NBA," HoopsHype.com, July 5, 2016, https://hoopshype .com/2016/07/05/how-the-warriors-got-kevin-durant-and-what-it -means-for-the-nba.

Darren Wolfson, "Wolves Owner: Butler Turns Down Extension, Towns Expected to Sign Extension," KSTP.com, July 13, 2018, https://kstp .com/sports/timberwolves-glen-taylor-jimmy-butler-contract -extension-karl-anthony-towns/4988445.

Mike Mullen, "Jimmy Butler Returns, Tells Timberwolves GM, 'You Fucking Need Me,'" *City Pages* (Minnesota), October 10, 2018, http://www.citypages.com/news/espn-jimmy-butler-returns-tells -timberwolves-gm-you-fucking-need-me/496683681.

Timothy Rapp, "Jimmy Butler Rumors: SG Wanted $155M Contract Before Trade Request," *Bleacher Report*, September 10, 2018, https://bleacherreport.com/articles/2796772-jimmy-butler-rumors -sg-wanted-155-million-contract-before-trade-request.

2018 NBA Western Conference First Round Timberwolves versus Rock- ets, BasketballReference.com, https://www.basketball-reference.com /playoffs/2018-nba-western-conference-first-round-timberwolves-vs -rockets.html.

Quoted in Ball-Rokeach and DeFleur, "A Dependency Model of Mass-Media Effects."

Chapter 12

Quoted in "Take That for Data: Basketball Analytics," MIT Sloane Sports Analytics Conference, Boston, February 2018, https://www.youtube .com/watch?v=jL2ZSMQOOS4.

Quoted in "NBA 2.0: New Rules to Transform the Game," MIT Sloane Sports Analytics Conference, Boston, February 2018, https://www.youtube.com/watch?v=RuxTtghwWgc.

Quoted in "Virgil Abloh—Return To The Air Jordan 1," interview, Air.

jordan.com, March 3, 2018, https://air.jordan.com/card/virgil-abloh -return-air-jordan-1.

Neil Paine, "Russell Westbrook Wasn't Supposed to Get Better Than Kevin Durant," FiveThirtyEight, February 18, 2016, https:// fivethirtyeight.com/features/russell-westbrook-wasnt-supposed -to-get-better-than-kevin-durant.

Quoted in "ESPN's Henry Abbott on TrueHoop, Serving Readers, and the Future of Sports Blogging," interview, Niemanlab.com, March 4, 2015, http://www.niemanlab.org/2014/03/qa-espns-henry-abbott -on-truehoop-serving-readers-and-the-future-of-sports-blogging.

Rick Maese, "NBA Embraces Advanced Analytics as Moneyball Move- ment Sweeps Pro Basketball," *Washington Post*, October 25, 2013, https://www.washingtonpost.com/sports/wizards/nba-embraces -advanced-analytics-as-moneyball-movement-sweeps-pro -basketball/2013/10/25/1bd40e24-3d7a-11e3-b0e7-716179a2c2c7 _story.html?utm_term=.62f88d887616.

Tim Bontemps, "Why NBA Stat Gurus Don't Really Hate Rudy Gay," *New York Post,* December 6, 2013, https://nypost.com/2013/12/06 /why-nba-stat-gurus-dont-really-hate-rudy-gay.

Terrance F. Ross, "Welcome to Smarter Basketball," *Atlantic*, June 25, 2015, https://www.theatlantic.com/entertainment/archive/2015/06 /nba-data-analytics/396776.

Ben Alamar, "Kyrie's Game 5 Performance Was a Mirage," ESPN Stats and Information Group, email, June 14, 2016.

Ben Cohn, "The Biggest Shot in NBA History," *Wall Street Journal*, December 25, 2016, https://www.wsj.com/articles/the-biggest-shot -in-nba-history-1482235610?mg=id-wsj.

John McTigue, "Warriors Too Much for Grizzlies in Game 1," ESPN Stats and Information Group, email, May 3, 2015.

Kyle Wagner, "Just What the Hell Is Real Plus-Minus, ESPN's New NBA Stat?" *Deadspin*, April 7, 2014, https://deadspin.com/just-what-the -hell-is-real-plus-minus-espns-new-nba-s-1560361469.

Nilkanth Patel, "Sam Hinkie and the Analytics Revolution in Basketball," *New Yorker*, May 17, 2013, https://www.newyorker.com/sports/sporting -scene/sam-hinkie-and-the-analytics-revolution-in-basketball.

Quoted in "Fear of Analytics," Marketing In Productivity blog http://blog.jimnovo.com/fear_analytics.

Michael Wilbon, "Mission Impossible: African-Americans and Analytics," *The Undefeated*, May 24, 2016, https://theundefeated.com /features/mission-impossible-african-americans-analytics.

Richard Pryor, *That Nigger's Crazy* (Partee/Stax Records, 1974).

Quoted in "Are 'Win Probabilities' Useless? ESPN's Director of Sports Analytics Says No," *USA Today*, February 22, 2017, https://www .usatoday.com/story/sports/ftw/2017/02/22/are-win-probabilities -useless-espns-director-of-sports-analytics-explains-why-theyre

–not/98250056.

Chapter 13

Newsweek, "I'm Not A Role Model," June 27, 1993, https://www.newsweek
.com/im-not-role-model-193808.

Shaun Harper, "Black NFL Players Should Exert Their Power," Hartford
Courant, May 26, 2018, https://www.courant.com/opinion/op-ed/hc
-op-harper-nfl-blacks-resist-anthem-policy-20180524-story.html.

Quoted in commercial for NBATickets.com, https://www.youtube.com
/watch?v=ATMk2uHKnz8.

Michael Singer, "Sacramento Kings Partner with Black Lives Matter amid
Stephon Clark Protests," *USA Today*, March 29, 2018, https://www
.usatoday.com/story/sports/nba/2018/03/29/sacramento-kings-partner
-black-lives-matter-amid-stephon-clark-protests/469290002.

Newswire, "Tom Gores Pledges $10 Million for Flint Relief Efforts,"
NBA.com, January 28, 2016, https://www.nba.com/pistons/news
/tom-gores-pledges-10-million-flint-relief-efforts.

Nelson Mandela, speech, Laureus Sports Awards 2000, May 25, 2000,
https://www.laureus.com/content/introduction-laureus.

Epilogue

Lauren W., "College Football's BEST Coaches of All Time!" Cleverst.com,
December 8, 2016, http://www.cleverst.com/sports/college
-best-coaches/45.

About the Author

Scoop Jackson is a national senior writer for ESPN. He has covered issues of race, culture, politics, and sports for various publications for over twenty-five years. He is the former executive editor of *XXL* and *Slam Magazine* and former publisher of the *Agenda*.

About Haymarket Books

Haymarket Books is a radical, independent, nonprofit book publisher based in Chicago.

Our mission is to publish books that contribute to struggles for social and economic justice. We strive to make our books a vibrant and organic part of social movements and the education and development of a critical, engaged, international left.

We take inspiration and courage from our namesakes, the Haymarket martyrs, who gave their lives fighting for a better world. Their 1886 struggle for the eight-hour day—which gave us May Day, the international workers' holiday—reminds workers around the world that ordinary people can organize and struggle for their own liberation. These struggles continue today across the globe—struggles against oppression, exploitation, poverty, and war.

Since our founding in 2001, Haymarket Books has published more than five hundred titles. Radically independent, we seek to drive a wedge into the risk-averse world of corporate book publishing. Our authors include Noam Chomsky, Arundhati Roy, Rebecca Solnit, Angela Y. Davis, Howard Zinn, Amy Goodman, Wallace Shawn, Mike Davis, Winona LaDuke, Ilan Pappé, Richard Wolff, Dave Zirin, Keeanga-Yamahtta Taylor, Nick Turse, Dahr Jamail, David Barsamian, Elizabeth Laird, Amira Hass, Mark Steel, Avi Lewis, Naomi Klein, and Neil Davidson. We are also the trade publishers of the acclaimed Historical Materialism Book Series and of Dispatch Books.

Also Available from Haymarket Books

Brazil's Dance with the Devil (Updated Olympics Edition)
The World Cup, the Olympics, and the Fight for Democracy
Dave Zirin

From #BlackLivesMatter to Black Liberation
Keeanga-Yamahtta Taylor

Freedom Is a Constant Struggle
Ferguson, Palestine, and the Foundations of a Movement
Angela Y. Davis, edited by Frank Barat, preface by Cornel West

The John Carlos Story
The Sports Moment That Changed the World
John Wesley Carlos and Dave Zirin
Foreword by Cornel West

Long Shot
The Triumphs and Struggles of an NBA Freedom Fighter
Rory Fanning and Craig Hodges, foreword by Dave Zirin

Things That Make White People Uncomfortable
Michael Bennett and Dave Zirin

Welcome to the Terrordome
The Pain, Politics, and Promise of Sports
Dave Zirin, foreword by Chuck D

What's My Name, Fool?
Sports and Resistance in the United States
Dave Zirin